WHEN THE MOON RISES

This photograph was taken near the summit of Monte Cimone (7100 ft) in October 1943, by an Italian photographer, a member of a band of partisans. The author is standing second from the left, Toby Graham fourth from the left and Michael Gilbert on the right. The others in the photograph, with the exception of the child, are deserters from the Alpini Regiment who later formed the nucleus of a partisan *banda*. The cylindrical object on the right is a gas cylinder mounted on the back of a *Volkswagen*.

When the Moon Rises

AN ESCAPE THROUGH WARTIME ITALY

by Tony Davies

WITH A FOREWORD BY
ERIC NEWBY

Leo Cooper
in association with
Secker & Warburg

First published in Great Britain 1973 by
LEO COOPER LTD
Republished 1985 by Leo Cooper,
in association with Secker & Warburg Ltd,
54 Poland Street, London W1V 3DF

ISBN 0 436 12450 5

Printed in Great Britain by
St Edmundsbury Press, Bury St Edmunds, Suffolk

CONTENTS

Foreword

I first met Tony Davies when, together with his companion-in-arms, Michael Gilbert, he emerged from the punishment cells at Campo P.G.21 after an extremely courageous attempt to escape from Italy in the spring of 1943, a feat which no allied prisoner of war succeeded in performing, so far as anyone knows, until after the Italian Armistice in September of the same year.

They had jumped from the window of a moving train at night and were very lucky to be alive, for train-jumping is one of the most hazardous methods of escaping : the take-off through the window has to be nicely judged, especially if there are telegraph poles along the line. These impediments and the presence of armed sentries in the corridor or the compartment itself, who are invariably sentenced to long terms of imprisonment if they fail to shoot straight, make the prospect for the jumper poor indeed and if two jump from the same compartment the prospect for the second is even worse.

Tony was tall and debonair as befitted an officer in a crack regiment of artillery, and thirty years later as a hardworking GP with a country practice he still is; but what really endeared him to me was his slightly loony appearance caused by a snaggle tooth, his infectious laugh which reminded me of Jack Hulbert giving an impromptu rendering of *The Flies Crawled up the Window* in the Casino at Monte Carlo before the war, and his incurable optimism, all of which survive to this day except the twisted front tooth which unfortunately was removed by a dental surgeon before I could clamp a preservation order on it.

Soon after their release from the cells we moved to a new camp further north at Fontanellato, a place so luxurious in comparison with any other camp we had so far inhabited that the wildest rumours circulated, the most acceptable being that we had been brought to it so that we might be fattened up and made sufficiently presentable to be exchanged for a similar number of Italian prisoners of war.

This, of course, was utter nonsense and so little believed by anyone in their right minds that escape attempts flourished and I found myself involved with Michael, whose brainchild it was, Tony and a number of others in the digging of a tunnel. It started on the first floor of the mock palazzo we inhabited and descended vertically through the solid brick-work of one of the piers which sprang from the floor of a crypt-like cellar in which we took our meals and which sup-ported the entire edifice so that when 'digging one's way to freedom' as some books would have it (not this one I am glad to say), one had the sensation while working at the face of being underground with one's feet in the air whereas one was actually poised in mid-air between the floor and the ceiling in the cellar. This dreadful, insensate labour was only brought to an end by the Armistice. I was in the prison hospital with Michael when the news came through. He had a huge carbuncle, I had a broken ankle and it was this that prevented me from accompanying Michael, Toby Graham and Tony on the great walk chronicled here. Reading it now, I think I had a lucky escape.

The next time I met Tony was in the wilds of Czecho-slovakia in 1944. Our paths had diverged for a time but one thing that we had both learned was the courage and human-ity of ordinary Italian people when everything seemed at its blackest and this is what *When the Moon Rises* is really all about.

Eric Newby,
Author of *Love and War in the Apennines.*
March, 1973.

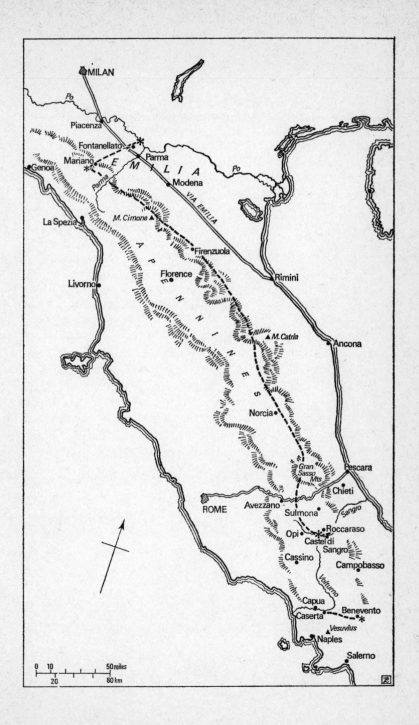

MILAN

Po

Piacenza

Fontanellato

Mariano

Parma

EMILIA

Genoa

Parma

Modena

Po

La Spezia

M. Cimone ▲

VIA EMILIA

Firenzuola

A

Florence

Rimini

Livorno

P

E

N

M. Catria ▲

N

I

Norcia

N

E

Gran
Sasso
Mts.

Pescara

S

Chieti

ROME

Avezzano

Sulmona

Sangro

Opi

Roccaraso

Castel di
Sangro

Cassino

Campobasso

Volturno

Capua

Benevento

Caserta

Vesuvius

Naples

Salerno

0 10   50 miles

20   80 km

2

PROLOGUE

Capture in Tunisia

Behind and above me in the light of the full moon rose
the shoulder of Two-Tree Hill, shorn of its characteristic topknot since being taken by the London Irish,
with appalling losses, a couple of days before. Below
and ahead, somewhere, lay the Germans, inspired with
renewed purpose since the arrival in Tunisia of General
von Arnim. It was 0200 on the morning of 16 January,
1943.

For the moment, as my signaller and I peered into
the moon's deep shadows, everything was peaceful. It
was one of those brief lulls which, in retrospect, are lent
a quite disproportionate significance by what happened
afterwards. At the time, crouched in the slit trench on
the forward side of the hill, and with memories of the
hard fighting of the previous few days still fresh in
mind, one was conscious of an equally deceptive,
though tightly-stretched, tranquillity. One hoped, but
did not quite believe, that the enemy had pulled back,
that we might be left in peace to recover and reform
after the mauling we had received.

This was the period immediately after the great
three weeks' rain, when the Allies, with a firm foothold
on the Algerian coast, had tried and failed to take

Tunis at a single stroke. The rain, grounding aircraft and halting tanks, had seen to that. Now, faced with a regrouped and determined German army, we seemed fated to fight out the winter in the Tunisian hills round Medjez-el-Bab. The Honourable Artillery Company Regiment, of which I was a junior member, had only been in North Africa for two months. We had left Britain in November and landed in Algiers after the first wave of the invasion was successfully ashore. From there we had been shipped by destroyer, under constant air attack, to Bone, where we had picked up our vehicles and joined up with the French Foreign Legion. There had been one or two skirmishes and a notable fiasco on Christmas Day before the line had been stabilized in the region of Medjez-el-Bab. A large-scale German tank attack had been successfully repulsed; and then, for three weeks of continuous downpour, we stuck. The RAF, with no all-weather airfields within reach, could not help us, and the Stukas plastered us regularly and without serious interference. It was a galling time.

Then came the assault on Two-Tree Hill. We were not directly involved, which in a way made it worse. The Germans were well dug in, and we watched the London Irish move slowly forward, being strafed by Heinkels, and suffering a steady drain of casualties. In the final attack, which took them to the summit and drove the enemy out, they were decimated.

It was because they were in such poor shape that I had been sent up with a signaller to help out as Forward Observation Officer. And there we were now, scanning the shadowed valley, with every nerve alert.

The sounds impinged on our senses only gradually; a low rumbling coming up from the darkness below us that steadily increased and became all too intelligible, the noise of armoured vehicles grinding up the hill towards us. I grabbed the field-telephone to inform Battery HQ, and at that moment the firing started, the darkness split apart by muzzle-flashes, the silence shattered by the roar of guns.

Then everything happened with sudden speed. A tank came lurching up and opened fire on my slit-trench. The signaller beside me was killed, and a second later I was hit in the back of the head. The impact sent me reeling. I was aware of blinding pain, and of copious blood pouring down my neck and soaking into my shirt. I lay where I had fallen, and I was quite certain that I was a goner.

As it turned out, I wasn't. The battle swept over and past—the Germans, patrolling in strength with armour, quickly recovered Two-Tree Hill and thereby completed the obliteration of the unfortunate London Irish—and in time I found myself being gently carried downhill by two German paras. Almost worse than death, I realized I was a prisoner.

This sounds like hyperbole, but it isn't. The Honourable Artillery Company, which traces its origins back to the Guild of St George established in the City of London in 1537, was one of the oldest and proudest formations one could belong to. The fact that the HAC is not part of the regular army but a militia regiment only serves to intensify its esprit de corps. It combined the battle readiness of the Guards with an almost Japanese preference for death rather than dishonour; and in the comparatively short time I had been with them I had become thoroughly inculcated with their special brand of pride.

Add to this a conventional public school upbringing,

which I had accepted without questioning, and in the disciplines of which I had been reasonably successful, and it may be understood that I was a mortally depressed individual as I was lugged downhill towards field hospital and captivity. As soon as I recovered— my wound turned out to be superficial, despite my premonitions of doom and death!—I had only one preoccupation, and that was to escape.

I spent eight days in a German hospital in Tunis. At the end of that time, when I was almost myself again, I, in common with all Allied prisoners captured in North Africa, was handed over to the Italians. It seemed that, as a result of an agreement between the Axis partners, we were to spend our captivity in Italy: there remained, however, the slight problem of getting us there.

PART ONE

Escape and Recapture

I

The prison cage was an enormous garage near the docks. There were about one thousand other prisoners there; five hundred British and five hundred French, the latter mainly Foreign Legion, but with a few Ghoums and other Colonial troops. The whole area had been wired off with a fence about twelve feet high and three feet wide. The wire was so thick one could hardly see through it, and outside it sentries were posted every ten yards—and a very touchy and trigger-happy bunch they were.

Inside the garage the prisoners loitered about or lay in groups. Few sights can be more pathetic than that of some hundreds of fit, active young men, formerly proud members of an efficient fighting force, disarmed and herded together like so many cattle at a market. I know my own feelings at this time were of intense misery and despair. The determination to seize the slightest chance of making a break—a chance which never in fact came—gradually gave way to desperation as the hours before embarkation slipped away. Had escape been possible, the odds on getting away with it would have been good. The Allies were rapidly building up their strength, and it could only be a matter of weeks before Tunis was taken and the Axis forces were cleared right out of Africa. Many of the civilians in Tunis must have realized this too, and I do not think they would have been averse to hiding a British soldier.

During the twenty-six hours I spent in the garage I explored every single square inch of the place, examined every crack and cranny, and watched the gate throughout the night, but not a glimmer of a chance came my way. And as I walked up the gang plank on to the ship next morning, I realized that if getting away from a temporary camp not far from the fighting line was difficult, then the chances of pulling off a successful escape from an established camp in an enemy country were likely to be a thousand times more so.

The ship was a merchantman of about two thousand tons with two large holds, one for'ard, one aft, and it appeared that the former had been reserved for the twenty or so British officers and the five hundred French prisoners. Previously it had been used for coal, and it was filthy, dark, damp and bitterly cold. There for three days we remained, in harbour, our only food a little ships' biscuit, our drink an occasional bucket of water lowered to us by our jeering and jubilant Italian guards and their doxies.

During these days I worked up a consuming hatred for the Italians; I could have throttled the life out of each one of those sentries and their women, and enjoyed it. Even now, years later, I seethe with anger at the memory of the squalor, degradation and bitterness of it all.

On the evening of the third day the hold was covered and battened down, leaving only a small gap of about a foot as an air hole; as the wedges were driven in it sounded for all the world like the nails being driven into a coffin lid.

The French, in their inimitable fashion, produced some candles, and their fitful light threw great shadows on the ship's plates. Later, the shuddering of the engines and the slight roll told us that our voyage had started.

At that time about fifty per cent of Italian shipping between Africa and Sicily was being sunk by the Royal Navy, the Fleet Air Arm, or RAF torpedo bombers. Had we been hit there was not the slightest chance of one of us getting out alive. The first night was uneventful; but the following morning the hold was uncovered, and the sentries told us that we were still in Tunis Bay waiting to pick up a destroyer escort.

During the second night I was woken from a doze by the sound of an enormous explosion, followed seconds later by the sudden lurching of the ship through an angle of about forty degrees. I was pitched forward on my face and rolled across the coal-dust. Then, slowly, the ship righted herself. At the same time there were panic-stricken shouts from above, and the sound of running feet. The staccato rattle of AA cannon shook the ship, and above this noise could be heard the roar of an aircraft. The French colonials thought the ship had been hit, and panicked accordingly.

During the whole attack I sat with my back against the side and kept my eyes fixed on a spot about thirty feet above, where I judged the water level to be, and I could swear I saw the plates burst asunder and the sea come rushing in to engulf us all. The entire episode couldn't have lasted more than three minutes, but when the echo of the last shot had died away I felt as though I had lived a lifetime in those moments: I was soaked in perspiration.

We docked at Naples the following morning, and after a further four hours' wait in the darkness the hatches were opened and we clambered up on deck, many of the men falling exhausted by the climb up the ladder. Five days on one dog biscuit is inclined to leave one feeling weak. Unshaven, with five days' growth of beard and as black as chimney-sweeps, we must have been a grim-looking bunch.

Italian guards, standing shoulder to shoulder, hustled us down the gangway on to the dockside; and it was during this performance that a very large Scots Guardsman suddenly decided he had had enough of being shoved around by these miserable little Italians. About halfway down, one of them made the mistake of clubbing him hard in the small of the back with his rifle butt: without a word, the Guardsman turned, picked him up, shook him, and then heaved him bodily over the side into the dock. Weak and miserable as we were, the sight of the sentry being fished out of Naples Dock on the end of a boathook cheered us up considerably. The remainder of the Italian guard—about five hundred strong—having overwhelmed the culprit, were screaming with rage and mortification. What should have been a grand show of strength, as they led their defeated enemy into captivity, had become a farce.

That evening we were taken by train to a transit camp at Capua on the Voltino river, about twenty miles north of Naples. To historians, Capua may conjure up visions of Roman glory in art and architecture—to me it will never be anything but the scene of Campo P.G. 66, a collection of tin-roofed shacks surrounded by a forest of barbed wire.

The camp consisted of a number of compounds each with its own wire fence, a series of prisons within a prison. At one time there must have been nearly ten thousand men there, most of them taken at Tobruk; and according to reports they had been through a very bad time. After the fall of Tobruk the Italian administrative services, never particularly efficient, had broken down altogether. Hundreds of British soldiers had died of thirst and disease in desert prison cages, due more, I think, to Italian inefficiency than to calculated cruelty. But the British ORs were adamant that the whole dismal story was as grim an 'Atrocity' as any hitherto perpetuated in the war, and they were after the blood of those responsible.

While the men had been left in desert cages to rot, the officers had fared better. They were flown out quickly, and Capua was one of the camps which housed them until they were moved on to permanent establishments. All the Tobruk prisoners had long since gone when I arrived, and the compound now contained about forty officers, all of them captured either in Tunis or on the 8th Army front in Tripoli.

To my great joy one of the first chaps I saw was Michael Gilbert—an old friend of mine from training days—alive and kicking and looking gaunter than ever. Michael had been sent out to investigate a farm which was believed to be in our hands. His driver had heard him talking to someone; and then a burst of automatic fire had come from the house. He didn't wait, but let in the clutch with a bang and shot off down the road in the darkness. As a result of his story, Michael was duly posted 'Missing' and most people were convinced that he was dead. It was wonderful to find a friend in the camp, and especially one whom I had expected never to see again. There was much to tell—and it was only now I realized how desperately tired I was. Michael and I went on yarning until I couldn't keep my eyes open any longer, and at last I went to bed and slept for forty-eight hours.

At the end of the first week I began to feel what it really meant to be a prisoner. The realization that for months, even years possibly, the greatest distance one could walk in any direction was just fifty yards, began to sink in. Standing in the compound and looking through the wire at the Italian countryside one could see fields and farms, peasants going about their business, and a road which disappeared round the shoulder of a hill. This feeling of being a caged animal is at its most acute for about the first three weeks—the 'wire-happy' stage, the older inhabitants called it—and it nearly drove me out of my mind. I spent every available moment pacing round the compound, gazing out at the world beyond the wire and eating my heart out with frustration and boredom. Luckily, this stage soon passes; and although one thinks and dreams of freedom during one's entire captivity, one learns to work out some philosophy to enable one to accept one's lot. And so POWs set about making themselves as comfortable as possible. They mend and wash their clothes and, once again, start to take some pride in their appearance. They talk incessantly with their comrades and indulge in interminable arguments over abstract and wonderful subjects, and become very cunning in the matter of making their rations edible. They make ingenious cooking stoves out of old jam tins, with which they are always brewing up something.

In our camp, the more scientifically-minded produced a forced-draught heater operated by a metal wheel turned by hand. When primed with wood or cardboard it gave out sufficient heat to boil a can of water very quickly indeed. The device was named proudly 'The Smokeless Heater'. Other less successful models were known as 'Heatless Smokers'; and I have seen men sitting on their haunches for an hour or more with their patent stoves, madly turning the metal wheel and stuffing the firebox with wooden chips and cardboard which it devoured like a starving beast. When at last they emerged from the smoke cloud, their eyes streaming and their faces black, they carried off their tins of lukewarm skilly to their bunks and ate the mess with as great a relish as if it had been created by Mrs Beeton herself.

Almost the entire day was spent preparing and cooking food. Eating it took very much less time; and because of the meagre rations, the subject of food was seldom out of our minds. We were not starving, but we were very hungry indeed. Breakfast consisted of a cup of black coffee made from dried lupin seeds. It tasted quite disgusting, but it was wet and warm. Lunch was a plate of macaroni soup and a roll of brown bread. Tea—a further cup of black coffee, with some cheese and a handful of dates. And that was that. The prisoners captured at Tobruk had existed for the whole winter on nothing else. On average each man had lost three stone in weight during those six months, but had managed to survive somehow.

Luckily for me, Red Cross food parcels had started to arrive at the camp by the time I got there. There was a shortage, so that one, designed to feed one man for one week, was shared between two; but we virtually lived off them, and although we were ravenously hungry all the time, so excellently balanced in food value were they, that most of us kept reasonably fit. Every Prisoner of War owes a debt of gratitude to the Red Cross; it is thanks to them that the majority of POWs in Europe were returned home still whole in mind and body.

3

Both Michael and I were desperately anxious to break out at the earliest possible moment, and gradually we began to work out a plan of campaign, as we made our interminable walks around the compound. Michael argued, quite rightly, that physical fitness was the first essential; and so we started our training by walking round the huts at a fast pace. At first we did twenty circuits, gradually increasing the distance so that after a week or two we were covering up to sixty circuits, and keeping up our speed.

We did most of our training after dark, between 7 and

9 p.m., firstly because the compound was reasonably deserted then, and we could scorch round the huts without hitting people; secondly, it was cooler; and thirdly, we could discuss our plans with a certain degree of secrecy. A prisoner who intends to escape very soon learns to keep his mouth shut. The minute he talks out of turn or is seen doing anything peculiar, he jeopardizes his chances. Not, usually, that he has anything to fear from his fellow prisoners—although I am sorry to say that isolated cases of treachery did occur—but as soon as one prisoner who is not actually in the scheme hears that something is on, then the whole camp knows about it. Our jailers were very good at detecting under-currents of this kind. Any change in our normally listless and aimless behaviour and they instinctively knew that something was going on and steps would be taken to prevent it. Michael and I therefore kept our own counsel and told no one what we were contemplating.

I think that most of those who have tried it will agree that any plan of escape can be divided into three stages. Stage 1—the actual break-out from the camp; Stage 2, the journey from the camp to the frontier or coast; and Stage 3, crossing the frontier and leaving the country. Which of these stages is the most difficult is a matter of opinion; all three can produce the most immense obstacles; but from my own experience I would say that the frontier crossing is the hardest. If he succeeds in getting that far, the fugitive is normally exhausted and his nerves are in a state of great tension. In fact, by that time he is near the end of his resources, and he is liable to make the kind of stupid mistakes he would certainly not make if he were fresh.

However, all three stages can be most difficult, and

in our case Stage 1 was proving damnably so. Any attempt at crossing the wire would be tantamount to suicide; the place was seething with sentries and they were all trigger-happy. The Italians regarded anyone trying to escape as completely mad; why else should they want to get out and get back to the war? Therefore such people were dangerous lunatics, quite capable of committing the most bloodthirsty crimes to attain their ends. I am sure that the average Italian sentry felt that a totally inadequate wire obstacle was the only thing between him and having his throat cut by rampaging Englishmen.

Tunnelling was impossible in such a restricted area; and Michael and I agreed that unless some irresistible opportunity presented itself in the meantime, our break would have to be made while we were being moved to our permanent camp—a move that could take place at any moment. Stage 1 was therefore pigeon-holed for the time being, and we concentrated on Stage 2.

Since the whole country was swarming with Germans, it occurred to us that this was the obvious mode of disguise. To the average Italian, the English and Germans look very much alike, since both are traditionally fair-skinned and tall; and we decided that broken Italian whether spoken by an Englishman or a German would sound atrocious to an Italian. Our few words of both languages would therefore probably see us through any encounter with the authorities, so long as our uniform was reasonably Germanic in appearance. Similarly, I feel sure that, at one stage of the war, a German soldier in his own uniform, slightly modified, could have walked unmolested down Piccadilly. Anyone interested enough to take any notice of him at all would probably have dismissed him as one of the innumerable foreign soldiers fighting on the Allied side. We hoped that the same reasoning would work for us.

Our main problem, therefore, was to alter our uniform, and this proved to be not nearly as difficult as we had imagined. The Afrika Korps tropical khaki drill was very similar to our own; and by sewing some red piping round the epaulettes and catching the trousers in at the ankle like skiing kit, we were able to produce a very tolerable imitation of it. With the addition of British boots and a leather belt apiece, we ought to pass as privates in the German Artillery. The only essential lacking was the vital peaked forage cap worn by Rommel's men; and here we had a stroke of luck. After struggling for two weeks to make one from strips of khaki drill taken from the pocket lining of our greatcoats and only succeeding in producing something like a French racing motorist's headgear, I happened to see, on the heads of two of the South African coloured troops in a neighbouring compound, as large as life, Afrika Korps caps. The problem now was how to get hold of them. The only time officers were ever taken out of their compound into the body of the prison was on sick parade, during which they had a chance of talking with the soldiers. A few whispered words to a corporal Paratrooper and things were well on the way. It would be easy enough, he said, to steal them, but we wanted no fuss, and so we asked him to bargain for them and tell us how the market stood on sick parade the following morning.

The price was not cheap: about a week's Red Cross food, two berets and—of all things—a string of beads. This last item nearly wrecked the entire transaction. We offered alternatives—food, money, anything we possessed—but no. Beads they wanted, and beads they were going to have. The situation was again saved by our invaluable Paratrooper. When I met him on the sick parade a few days later he manoeuvred himself alongside and produced a string of brilliantly coloured beads. I never asked him how he got them, but I rather imagine some other unfortunate South African had 'lost' them some dark night. The deal was rapidly completed, and the caps were duly handed over during sick parade and smuggled back into the officers' compound.

This Paratrooper was typical of the ORs I met in captivity. He never once asked us why we wanted the hats, but he obviously realized we were working on some scheme and he helped us without question or hesitation.

Now things were really beginning to take shape. Our rough plan of campaign after the immediate break-out was to walk the eighty odd miles to the Adriatic coast, steal a boat from some fishing village, sail to Jugoslavia and contact the partisans and the British Military Mission operating with them. We would walk at night and lie up in the country during the day. We had maps —copies of the silk escape maps issued to the Paratroops, which they had successfully smuggled through two or three searches—and a little money.

Money was the most essential commodity to a would-be escaper, and it was the most difficult to get. About the only method was by bribing the sentries with Red Cross food or cigarettes, and the price was dirt cheap—to them. My small supply was hidden in a large tin of 'Germolene' ointment, which I had carried with me ever since I left England and which had not been taken from me when I was captured. The lira were wrapped in cellophane and pressed into the tin, which was then

warmed gently until the ointment melted. When left
to cool, it set hard again, leaving a smooth surface
beneath which the money lay concealed. This defied
numerous searches; and as I obtained more money so
I acquired more tins of ointment. Eventually, in
addition to my original Germolene, I had six tins of
Italian cold cream—all crammed with my precious
lira.

We estimated that our proposed journey would take
us about a month, and we started preparing iron
rations to cover this period. We intended to live off the
country as much as possible, but although fruit and
vegetables would be easy to come by, a reasonable
protein intake would not, and so we set about making
our own to take with us. Each week we set aside some
of the more nourishing food from our Red Cross
parcels—a fearful discipline when one is perpetually
famished. The sugar, condensed milk, bacon fat,
margarine, cocoa and raisins we thus hoarded were
thoroughly mixed, heated, and poured into a series of
Rowntree's oblong cocoa tins. Then we sealed them to
cool. The results tasted quite nice or completely foul,
depending on the amount of bacon fat; but they set
hard and remained edible months later.

Why go to these lengths, you may wonder, to make
portable iron rations when tinned food from the Red
Cross was available anyway? The answer is that the
Italians, realizing the value of unopened tins to those
contemplating escape, pierced every one as each parcel
was issued.

We then proceeded to make cloth belts with pouches
to hold the ration tins. These belts we put on under our
jackets, and, with the weight properly distributed, they
were very little hindrance. The increased waistline was

hardly noticeable, and on the whole we were reasonably satisfied with our efforts.

So far, so good. We had money, maps and a supply of food, an excellent disguise and a reasonable plan once we were out. But for the moment we were still in; and all we could do was to wait for the move to a permanent camp—wait, keep fit, and tie up any loose ends.

4

Time dragged on, and the monotony of our lives nearly drove us distracted.

Then one morning, after I had been at Capua for about six weeks, the Italian orderly officer taking the first roll-call informed us that a party of about forty officers was to be moved to a permanent camp that afternoon. Michael and I were included, and so we spent the morning feverishly packing our kit and hiding on our persons our maps, money and other essentials. It was vital to our project that we should get through the search on leaving camp, and, by all accounts, it was likely to be a tough one. The caps were concealed beneath our pants; the maps were sewn into our vests between the shoulder blades, and my precious hoard of ointments and the cocoa tins were tucked into our belts with remnants of other opened, half-eaten tins of Red Cross food.

We were paraded at three in the afternoon, and then moved out of the camp and into the search hut. For a whole hour, and with a mouth as dry as dust, I was subjected to an examination which any British Customs and Excise man would have watched with professional admiration; but eventually my baggage was metaphorically chalked up and I moved outside. Not a thing had I lost. Michael joined me. He, too, had been lucky, and as we moved off down the road to the station we felt that the gods were on our side.

The march to the station must have been a wonderful sight. The forty of us, each carrying his few possessions with him, were escorted by nearly as many soldiers—tiny little men most of them—who found the pace set by our leading file a bit too much for them. We lengthened our stride, settling down to a good 120 paces to the minute, and soon the escort had to break into a trot to keep up. By the time we reached the station the majority were running quite hard, with their slung rifles clattering and banging their spurs and the perspiration running down their faces. We were far from popular, and were bundled into carriages at bayonet-point to the accompaniment of curses from the sentries and hisses from a crowd of civilians who had witnessed our marathon through the main streets of the town.

At that time the Italians took a great pride in their army and in the achievements of their soldiers, whom they referred to affectionately as 'I Nostri', or 'I Nostri piccoli' (Our little ones). To describe a national army as 'Our little ones' struck the average British soldier as highly ludicrous. The Italians are not a martial people, and their affection for their army was occasioned not by feats of gallantry on the battlefield, but by a natural sympathy for anyone unfortunate enough to be caught in the draft and unable to wangle his way out. I doubt if there is any race who looked upon soldiering with such distaste, but who, once the uniform was donned, gloried so much in the pomp and splendour of it. Never did any army shout more and shoot less—which may explain the Italians' hatred for the Germans and the Germans' contempt of the Italians.

One thing no Italian can bear is to be held up to ridicule; and since it was extremely easy to make these soldiers look ridiculous, we naturally incurred the wrath of all who had witnessed our arrival at the station. We sat in the train with everyone—from the officer commanding the escort to the tiniest child in the crowd—screaming abuse and insults at us.

The carriages were the normal second class coaches of the Italian State Railways, with corridors. There were six officers to each compartment with a sentry standing in the doorway. The only exits were the two doors, one at each end of the corridor. Michael and I were lucky enough to secure the two seats by the window. These windows, which we were forbidden to open, could be pulled right down by two handles, giving an aperture about three feet square—plenty big enough for a man to get through.

We eventually pulled out of Capua at about six o'clock in the evening. Our destination was a large permanent officers' camp at Chieti, near Pescara on the Adriatic coast, about one hundred miles away, and it was obvious that the greater part of the journey would take place at night. Our route was due south for a few miles to the junction at Caserta, near Naples, and then north-east from there on the long haul over the mountains. Darkness had fallen by the time the train left Caserta and began the climb.

Our sentry was at last relaxing a little, and no longer clutched his rifle as if at any moment it was going to be snatched from him. We assisted the process by offering him cigarettes, which he took gratefully after a glance down the corridor to see if he was observed, and chatting to him with the few words of Italian we knew. Soon he was quite at his ease, leaning against the side of the doorway and with his rifle propped against his legs. Three of the other officers in the carriage had fallen asleep, and everything appeared calm and peaceful.

Michael and I had long since arranged our gear. Our belts of iron rations were strapped on, and our pockets were stuffed with one or two additional small tins and some chocolate. Our money and maps were securely stowed. We had been able to arrange all this without attracting the sentry's attention, thanks to the guard's decision to extinguish the lights in the compartments while keeping those in the corridor on. This meant that the sentry was standing in the light and peering into the dark, so that while we could see every move he made, I doubt if he could see us at all. No arrangement could have suited our purpose better. With the silence in the compartment broken only by the snores of those asleep, and the wheels clicking their way through the mountains, we settled down to wait for a suitable moment to go.

This waiting was the worst part of the whole business, and as I sat in my corner with as much composure as I could muster, my knees felt like water and my stomach quite hollow. Time and again I was convinced that the ideal spot had arrived and was just tensing myself to leap when with a 'woosh' and a sigh the train plunged under a bridge or into a tunnel. After each of these episodes I had a distinct vision of my body hurtling against the bridge parapet, or falling like a sack into the river bed hundreds of feet below. Eventually I was sweating with apprehension and could happily have called the whole thing off.

All this time the train had been climbing into the mountains at a steady thirty miles an hour; but now, to our horror, we felt her start to accelerate. That could only mean we were on a down gradient. If we were going to jump at all, now was the time. I kicked the chap next to me, who was in on the plan. He rose and offered the sentry a cigarette. Standing with his back to us, he struck a match and shielded it in his cupped hands while he and the sentry lit up. Mike tapped my boot, and, in one movement, pulled down the window and was gone. I followed. As I heaved myself over the window and hung there by my hands for a second, I had a momentary view of the sentry's face as the match illuminated it. Then, pushing hard with my legs against the side of the carriage, I dropped. In the next few seconds I hit the ground at least twice, rolled over and over and eventually came to rest in the middle of a small road that ran beside the track. I picked myself up and tore up the hillside—scrambling over rocks and falling through bushes—and even as I did so I heard the scream of the wheels on metal as the engine braked, and the shots from the sentries. The soldiers on the flat van at the rear of the train must have seen us go.

When I had put about four hundred yards between myself and the railway line I stopped, crouching in the shadow of a large rock. The moon was up by this time, and visibility was excellent, but the silvery whiteness of the country was accentuated by the dark shadows cast by rocks on the hillside. So, in the shelter of this darkness, I regained my breath, my chest stopped heaving, and I could watch with a certain amount of detached amusement the scene going on below. I was perfectly safe. A handful of soldiers hadn't a hope of catching me in that rocky wilderness.

At first there appeared to be complete pandemonium around the stationary train. Men were shouting and gesticulating, and there seemed to be a first-class argument in progress. After some minutes a party of six or seven started to pick their way up the mountain towards me. Their progress was very slow and hesitating; they quite obviously didn't like the idea of sweating up a steep mountainside in the rather forlorn hope of catching two desperate characters!

The noise from the train grew louder, and the sound of cheering, and 'God Save the King', came floating up from the valley. The boys were creating a frightful din, and very soon it had the desired effect. The Italians called off the hunt and the sentries returned to the train. It must have suddenly occurred to them that they were in grave danger of losing the entire train-load of prisoners in the confusion and consternation caused by our jump.

The singing and shouting gradually died down and the train moved off slowly, gathering speed. Within a few minutes the only sound to be heard was the gentle splashing of a stream as it tumbled its way down the mountain.

5

I don't suppose I shall ever again experience a feeling of such elation and joy as at the moment, when the full realization that I was once more a free man broke upon me. I wanted to sing and dance. I did shout two or three times at the top of my voice 'I'm free—I'm free!' I felt a hell of a chap, and very very proud of myself.

After a few minutes of this self-congratulation I came down to earth again. The first thing to do was to contact Michael. He must be somewhere fairly close, as we had planned to meet at a point about four or five hundred yards away from the scene of the jump. I stood up and looked around. I was about half-way up a steep re-entrant leading to the crest above, no more than two hundred yards wide. A spur of the hill projected from the crest which formed one side of the gully in which I was standing, and sloped down to the road and railway. On the other side was another spur, so that I was really placed in a narrow defile at one end by the crest of the mountain above.

I started to call for Michael, softly at first and then more loudly. But when the echo of my voice died away, not a sound did I hear. I moved farther up the defile and on to the crest of the spur, and for half an hour I bellowed Michael's name at the top of my voice, but my only answer was the distant barking of a dog, coming crystal clear through the stillness of the night.

For at least an hour I explored the area. I went down to the railway track and along the road for nearly half a mile. I wondered if he had hurt himself badly in the jump—broken a leg maybe—and was lying in some ditch unable to move and too weak to answer my shouts. But I found nothing, and at last was forced to admit that from now on I was on my own. I climbed up the re-entrant to the crest above, and there sat down to take stock of my position.

I at once made a depressing discovery: to my dismay I found that about ninety per cent of my food had gone; scattered, presumably, over the ground where I had landed. The pouch belt had been a complete failure, for it had broken adrift during the initial fall. Now my entire stock consisted of one very small tin of cheese and a bar of chocolate. Money, cigarettes, food—all had gone as surely as if I had turned my pockets inside out; and, to crown everything, the right leg of my drill trousers was torn from thigh to ankle. My leg had bled considerably from a jagged cut, and was beginning to stiffen. Each of us had provided ourselves with a needle and cotton, and so, for the next twenty minutes I perched my bared anatomy on a small stone, and, in the bright moonlight, solemnly repaired my trousers.

Then I removed the maps from my vest and tried to fix my position. Vesuvius was glowing away in the distance and the whole countryside, bathed in the whiteness of the moonlight, presented a picture of great beauty. According to my map, a main railway line from Naples to the Adriatic coast ran about five miles to the north through a wide valley which very nearly traversed the mountain from east to west. To reach it I should have a river to cross, but that problem I decided to deal with when it came. It was quite obvious that our original plan of walking the hundred odd miles to the Adriatic coast was now out of the question, owing to the shortage of food, and that my only hope of success was to get as far as possible by train. I decided, therefore, to reach the main line during the night, board a train and be out of the area before the hue and cry started up again in the morning. So be it. I straightened my uniform, donned my Afrika Korps cap, and moved off along a narrow mule track which twisted and turned its way over the mountains, now plunging steeply into a valley, and now climbing tortuously up a cliff face.

After two hours of this difficult going, the country became less desolate and rugged, and the track led down through terraced, cultivated land dotted with farm houses. I approached these signs of civilization with a certain amount of apprehension, and passed the houses by taking a wide detour round each one. I moved as noiselessly as I could, walking on grass where possible, and avoiding the stone and gravel paths. Even so, the dogs knew someone was about, and they would follow me from farm to farm, barking and yelping fit to wake the dead. Soon the entire neighbourhood resounded with their frantic noise, and only by running until my lungs were on the point of bursting did I manage to shake them off.

By this time I had reached a fairly good motor road, and after the rocks and hills of the previous two hours, the going was delightfully easy and I clipped along at a good pace. I passed through two or three villages. In each case I removed my boots and padded through in my socks; but there was not a sound or movement to reveal that they were inhabited. The only sign of life in all this time was one large army vehicle. I heard the hum of its engine and saw the beam of its headlights cut into the darkness of the village street, and just had time to dart into the doorway of a shop. Pressing myself as far back as I could, I watched it pass and heard it fade into the night.

Shortly after this, to my great relief, I found myself in open country again. I felt a lot safer away from those narrow village streets, and put on my boots again and stepped out briskly. I reckoned I still had quite a way to go to the railway, and it was already after 2 a.m. I had only about two and a half hours of darkness left. I should also be approaching the river very soon; but there was no sign or sound of water. The first doubts as to whether I was on the right road began to creep into my mind, and I was just about to sit down and take another look at my map, when round a sharp corner, not a hundred yards away, were the river and the bridge. Three soldiers were sitting round a brazier by the side of the road, bathed in the light which shone from the guard hut behind them. Inside I could see a few forms rolled in blankets, a wooden table and a row of rifles stacked against the wall. The three men around the brazier were completely shrouded in blankets, which they wore like shawls. They were chatting quietly, and seemed completely oblivious of everything except the glowing fire.

Crouching in the shadow of the bank, I watched them for several minutes, trying to decide what to do next. The river itself was a raging torrent some hundreds of feet below in a gorge. The bridge over it was, in fact, a viaduct, and I was reminded of the famous bridge in Ernest Hemingway's *For Whom the Bell Tolls*. With a small force of men, how easy it would be to destroy it. It was to combat any possibility of such an attack by parachute forces that all bridges in Southern Italy were guarded.

After much vacillation I eventually decided to try

and cross the bridge quite openly. After all, I must look like a German soldier, and the uniform was sufficiently authentic to fool the average Italian. With as much confidence and arrogance as I could muster, therefore, I stepped into the middle of the road and marched towards the sentries, softly whistling *Lili Marlene* between my teeth. As I drew level with the three men I gave them a quiet '*Gute Nacht*' which they acknowledged with rather surly nods, and then I was on the metal bridge, my steel-tipped heels making a fearful noise as I stomped across. Not a sound, not a challenge followed me. I was almost half-way across when I heard running feet and an excited voice shouting at me in Italian. I stopped and turned round. The sentry caught up with me, talking and pointing all the time. I noticed that his rifle was still slung, and it soon became apparent that he was trying very hard to tell me something. I hadn't the faintest clue what he was talking about, and in a mixture of broken German and Italian told him so.

'*Tedesco, io non capisco. Verstehen, sie?*' At last, after much pointing, and with the aid of his companion who had come up to us by this time, I began to understand what he was driving at. Please would I not make so much noise with my feet crossing the bridge as I should wake up those sentries asleep in the huts at either end and then the Sergeant of the Guard would himself come out and make them patrol the bridge instead of sitting in comfort round the brazier.

I was so relieved to know that this was all they wanted, and that they had no suspicion of my real identity, I could have laughed outright. Instead, I mimed profuse apologies, and within minutes we were all the greatest of friends. I gave them a little of my chocolate and in return was given a packet of those foul Italian cigarettes, 'Milits'; and with much winking and talk of the attractions of women who could make men walk miles back to their own beds in the small hours of the morning, we parted on the best of terms. My step lightened; I chortled with glee. My confidence knew no bounds. This whole thing was going to be an absolute cake-walk. I couldn't possibly go wrong.

I reached the railway as dawn was breaking and walked alongside the track until a station appeared. It was on the outskirts of a fair-sized village, and already, at five o'clock in the morning, there seemed to be quite a crowd waiting for a train. Most of them were peasants, chatting around a small fire in the waiting room, but among them I saw a few soldiers. The station lights were still on, and a shaft from the open door of the waiting room shone across the track. At one end of the platform there was a small square building with 'Donne' on one door and 'Uomini' on the other. I made a bee-line for this haven and entered the right part of it—unlike another escaped prisoner who had unfortunately tried the door marked 'Donne' and found himself arrested for indecency. On such minor mistakes many a bid for freedom has come to grief.

The interior of this insalubrious place was in an indescribable state and the smell was appalling. However, it housed the essentials, and so I washed and examined my face in a mirror. In spite of a stubbly chin, I considered that I looked quite presentable.

I was careful to avoid looking surreptitious and openly walked up and down the platform while I waited for the train. There is much wisdom, for those on the run, in the adage 'Feel hunted and you'll look hunted'. I tried my utmost therefore to live the part I was playing, and to behave like a German soldier returning from a night on the binge. The Italian civilians seemed to go out of their way to avoid me, and showed very little interest. An Italian sergeant, however, complete with kit and rifle and obviously fresh from leave, was inclined to be friendly. He dumped his kit and fell into step beside me, and together we paced slowly up and down, conversing in an odd mixture of Italian, French and German.

The encounter proved to be invaluable. Up to that moment I hadn't been sure which way the tracks ran; but now the sergeant told me he was returning to Naples, and that his train was due in a few minutes. The inevitable question then arose, 'And where are you going? Naples, perhaps? Or Caserta?'

'No,' I said, and indicated the other direction.

The Italian then brought out a whole string of town names—San Lorenzo, Finoli, Benevento, and so on. Picking one of them at random, I told him Benevento was the place.

'Ah,' he said, 'then you are on the wrong platform. Your train comes in on that side and is due in about half an hour.' I thanked him for his help and stayed chatting with him until his train arrived, when we wished each other goodbye and good luck. I needed it.

6

I crossed to the other platform and in due course my train arrived. I opened the door of an empty coach and got in. The whole train seemed deserted; I settled myself in a corner seat and waited. After a time three civilians entered, saw me in the compartment, and immediately chose seats as far away as possible. During the next ten minutes the coach was half filled, with the Italians crowded at one end, and myself in splendid isolation at the other. How they loved their German allies!

I stared out of the window and smoked a cigarette. My nervousness was increasing while the train was stationary, and I expected the police to appear at any moment and haul me off. It was now broad daylight, and I was becoming increasingly aware of the inadequacies of my disguise.

At last, after what seemed hours of waiting, the train slowly pulled out of the station, and I breathed more freely. My biggest trial was yet to come, however, for I had no ticket and no money; and I was still trying to decide what my best course of action would be when the guard appeared. In little local trains the guard is like a tram conductor, issuing tickets on the spot or punching those obtained at the stations.

He approached my end of the compartment.

'Biglietto, per favore.' I glowered at him.

'Niente,' I said, 'E perduto. I've lost it.'

'Where are you going?'

'To Benevento, but it's no use your standing there because I haven't any money.' I looked at him hard and with as great a show of arrogance as I could muster. He hesitated for a moment—was about to say something, then thought better of it, and, muttering under his breath, he gave an expressive shrug of the shoulders and went on into the next coach. Strange as it may seem, this was quite typical of the Italians' outlook on life; their creed appeared to be 'Anything for peace and quiet'. It may have been reinforced, in this case, by their fear and loathing of their German masters.

My luck was holding. Sheer effrontery was the answer, and my optimism mounted. I felt I was going to get away with it; and, secure in this comforting conviction, I settled down, quite at ease, to enjoy the journey.

I lit one of my Italian cigarettes and gazed out of the window at the Abruzzi countryside. Our progress through it was by no means headlong. At every station we stopped for five or ten minutes, and gradually the compartment filled up. After about an hour of this the only unoccupied seats in the entire coach were the one next to mine and the two opposite. Beyond this 'cordon sanitaire' it was filled with a noisy, chattering crowd of Italian peasants. But as the train jolted to a halt at the next station I saw a very different type of passenger on the platform—some twenty or thirty of them—shouting, jostling their way on to the train with their satchels on their backs and school books under their arms. There was a mad scramble into the compartment, and three of them flung themselves into the vacant seats around me. They were as high-spirited and noisy as schoolboys the world over; but two of them, I noticed, were wearing the ridiculous black monkey hats of the 'Giovani Fascisti'. I was immediately on my guard. Children generally are sharp-eyed and inquisitive, and these two particularly, with their open allegiance to the régime, would be more likely than most to spot any short-comings in my uniform.

Sure enough, they started to ask questions almost as soon as they had sat down. One of them I took a particular dislike to, a tall spotty youth of about fifteen; and he shattered me completely by addressing me in what sounded like very fluent German. His companions looked at him with a certain amount of awe and tittered while they waited for my reply. Here, I thought, was obviously the bright boy, the school linguist, who was enjoying the chance of showing off to his friends.

'I don't understand you,' I said to him in Italian, 'but if you wish to speak to me, speak in Italian—it is easier for both of us.'

There was a moment's silence; the spotty youth blushed scarlet and then his companions shouted with laughter, pointing and jeering at him. Poor wretch, I very nearly felt sorry for him. The one time he has a chance of speaking to a real German in his own language, the German can't understand a word he says! I'll bet he took a long time to live that down.

However, not wishing to antagonize these youngsters, I gave them a little of my chocolate and, in my mixture of Italian and German, discussed with them the war, and the great German Army, and the great Italian Army, and the British Army which, according to them, was made up entirely of black troops and Indians. I shot them a tremendous line about the Afrika Korps and Rommel, but was hard put to it to explain away the imminent defeat of the Axis forces in North Africa. By the time they reached their destination we were the best of friends.

As they got out of the train, they told me that it would be at Benevento in another ten minutes. With the imminent prospect of trying to bluff my way through the ticket barrier and possibly a swarm of military police, I lost some of my bounce, and I waited in a sweat of apprehension. The journey had taken me over a hundred miles nearer my goal; but I had been sitting in the same seat for the best part of four hours, and for that reason, at least, I was not sorry it was over.

Benevento's main claim to importance is its distillery, which became well known to the British soldiers who later landed in Italy. After the liberation of the city, it was put to work at high pressure producing vast quantities of gin. Judging from the number of tracks running into the station, Benevento was also a major railway junction. The platforms were crowded with civilians and soldiers, and, to my anxious eyes as I peered through the window, there appeared to be a great number of Carabinieri—State police—gathered at each exit. I left the coach and mingled with the crowd queuing to pass through the barrier, and even as I did so I could see out of the corner of my eye the police speaking to the train guard and searching the compartments. At the barrier every passenger was being subjected to a very close scrutiny, and in some cases the police were demanding to see papers. It was quite obvious that this was no routine check but a systematic examination of all passengers leaving trains. The authorities were on the alert; and I had no doubt at all that the object of their search was myself.

I left the queue as unobtrusively as I could and sauntered along the platform to the gents. Here I shut myself in a closet. By standing on tiptoe I could see out of the window and keep an eye on affairs outside. I waited for what seemed like hours, while the crowd dwindled and the platform emptied. The police moved across the track to another platform and repeated the procedure with passengers alighting from a train that pulled in from the opposite direction.

I watched the arrival and departure of three more trains, and in each case every passenger was thoroughly checked and the coaches searched. I could see no way of getting away from the station without being caught in the net, and was preparing myself like the 'three old ladies' for a long stay in my sanctuary, when salvation, in the form of a German troop train, appeared. There were about two hundred soldiers on board, and with much barking of orders from the RTO the whole battalion detrained and formed up on the platform. A party of twenty men were detailed to deal with the baggage wagon, while the remainder marched off through the station and into the town.

The baggage team took their time over the unloading, and men would wander off up the platform and through the barrier to the refreshment room. Occasionally one or two would answer the call of nature and I would hear them whistling to themselves or chatting on the other side of the door. Choosing my moment, I slipped out of the lavatory, and with my sleeves rolled up and puffing a cigarette I strolled along the platform and through the barrier. The Carabinieri did no more than nod a salutation. In a matter of seconds I was out of the station and in the street.

As soon as I was out of sight I quickened my pace, and presently reached the comparative sanctuary of the main square. Here women with shopping baskets on their arms were chatting, cars and trams rattled over the cobbled streets, and children were sucking ice cream cornets. I might have been in any English market town. Surrounded by this mass of humanity I felt safer and less conspicuous; and although my heart gave a jolt at the sight of a policeman, my confidence and optimism quickly returned.

My intention at this time was to cross the town and pick up the rail track again at a point about ten miles east of Benevento. Here I hoped to repeat the pattern of my previous journey, this time gaining the Adriatic coast a further forty miles north-east.

I was beginning to feel appallingly hungry, and after taking a long drink of water at a public fountain I allowed myself one small square of chocolate. My supply was dwindling fast, and I began to regret my generosity to the bridge sentry the night before, and to the boys in the train; but I consoled myself with the thought that what I had given away would have made very little difference to my appetite.

From time to time as I made my way to the outskirts of the town I caught sight of the odd German soldier; but by keeping my eyes open, and by skilful manoeuvring, I avoided meeting one of them face to face. At the same time I didn't much like the look of things. I hadn't bargained for meeting genuine members of the German army and I knew full well that any direct contact between us would end in disaster. There was plenty of evidence that a large German formation was in or near the city. There were numerous traffic signs, Military Police notices, and all the other threats and exhortations which military authorities post up for the benefit of the soldiers everywhere in the world. However, as I left the town centre and reached what appeared to be a rather squalid residential area, these signs of German activity became fewer and eventually disappeared altogether.

The street I was in now was typical of the working-class area of any Italian town. Tall tenement buildings lined both sides, and made it appear narrower than it really was. Slogans were scrawled on every available piece of wall: 'Viva il Duce', 'Vinceremo' and 'Roma Roma' glared at one at every turn. The cobbled street itself was filthy, and garbage was piled up in the gutters. The whole place had a quite specific smell.

More to the point, this canyon of workers' apartments had not a single turning or side street off it. I was striding out along it when, round a blind bend no more than fifty yards away, a company of German infantry came marching towards me.

In the next few seconds I made the one vital mistake. If I had turned and run I might possibly have got away with it, but I decided to carry straight on and bluff it out. I kept to my side of the road, looking straight ahead and marching with as Teutonic a bearing as I could muster, scarcely daring to breathe. Twenty yards, ten yards, the company drew abreast. I didn't glance at them and I must have been nearly fifty yards beyond when I heard the shouted command and the formation halted. Then there were running feet behind me and a torrent of excited German.

'Hallo—Halten Sie—Halt!' I halted.

The NCO in command of the company, a Feldwebel, and two soldiers stood facing me. The soldiers had their rifles lowered, and the NCO screamed abuse at me as only a German can. I didn't understand a word but I got the impression that he was arresting me as a deserter. And then, in the middle of this diatribe he stopped. He peered at my uniform, and then burst into laughter. In very passable English he said:

'You are one of the two British officers who escaped from the prison train. Yes?'

In either case I was under arrest, and I saw no future in being held as a deserter.

'You are quite right.' I said.

'In that case, Herr . . . ?' and he hesitated, waiting.

'Oberleutnant.'

'In that case, Herr Oberleutnant, you are my prisoner and will accompany me. It would be better,' he said, 'not to give the escort trouble.'

I looked at the escort, two oafish youths, and I had to agree with him. It would be better not to give the escort trouble.

7

The Feldwebel placed the company under command of another NCO and the main body moved off, leaving him, the escort and myself to march back into the town independently. I was feeling desperately dejected, and cursed myself for a fool. If only, instead of trying to bluff things out, I had cut and run for it, I might still be a free man. If only . . .

Now the tension was over and I began to be aware of a great weariness, mental as well as physical, and also of intense hunger. The Feldwebel was enjoying himself and was in an expansive mood. He chattered away gaily, slapping his thigh with merriment at the thought of a British officer dressed as a German hoodwinking the Italians.

'You are a brave man, Herr Oberleutnant,' he

said. 'Escaping is a highly dangerous business, and to be successful requires great courage and skill. Your attempt commands my admiration, and although we are enemies we can shake hands on it.' Here he stopped, grasped my hand and shook it vigorously. Then, clicking his heels, he gave me a salute. I felt a perfect idiot, though I could understand his good humour and amusement. He was likely to be commended for apprehending an escaped prisoner—especially since the prisoner had eluded all attempts by the Italians to recapture him. He asked me where my companion was, and seemed quite satisfied when I told him I had no idea. Whether he believed me or not, I can't say, but the fact that he asked meant that Michael was still at large. I was delighted—if a little jealous!

'You know,' he said, 'the funniest thing about this whole business is that the Italians have called out at least a division to look for you. You are classed as highly dangerous and to be recaptured at all costs. What a joke! You dodge the whole lot of them and walk straight into me. Funny, isn't it?' I looked at him with a baleful glare.

'You appear to find it so,' I said with great bitterness.

'Ah well,' he said, 'cheer up. There will probably come another time for you. Meanwhile, why should you worry—the war for you is over.'

We stopped at a small *ristorante* where he ordered vino and some minestrone and spaghetti for me. He watched me closely as I bolted the food down.

'You must have been very hungry,' he said. 'Don't the Italians feed you well?' I told him in a few short well-chosen words.

'Well, what can you expect of such a nation? It is your great misfortune that you were not sent to

Germany when you were captured. We treat our prisoners well and respect the Geneva Convention.

I had no knowledge of German prison camps, but I was extremely thankful not to be in one. It was obvious, even at this time, that Italy's days in the war were numbered, and that capitulation or invasion would probably bring my captivity to an end long before it would have done in Germany.

At last the Feldwebel rose from the table, and said, 'Now, Herr Oberleutnant, I very much regret that I shall have to hand you over to the Italian authorities. I have no alternative.' And with that our little party set off again, and I was solemnly marched through the town and into the Italian Military Police headquarters. With much arrogance and blustering, he announced my capture, and then sent an Italian soldier off to fetch me a chair. He waited until an officer arrived and the formalities were completed. Then, once again, he clicked his heels and saluted.

'Auf Wiedersehen, Herr Oberleutnant.' He turned smartly and was gone.

Within minutes the room was full of people, soldiers, Carabinieri—even a civilian or two—all peering at me and gabbling away. There was much clicking of tongues and shaking of heads, and I felt ridiculously like a schoolboy who has done something wrong. There was very little hostility, which surprised me, and the whole atmosphere was mainly of curiosity. Eventually an interpreter arrived. He was quite young, and he might well have stepped straight out of a Soho restaurant. Throughout the interrogation that followed, I listened, fascinated, to his Cockney accent. The Italian officer conducting the enquiry kept asking why I had escaped.

'You go through the hell of Africa, and the beastliness of fighting; you are fortunate enough to be captured and to leave all that behind you. You come to our lovely country, and then, at the first opportunity, you risk your life so that you can get back to the war. You must be crazy!'

To finish the conversation I agreed with him.

'Yes, I'm crazy,' I said wearily, and this seemed to satisfy him, for the interrogation ended there.

As I sat dozing in the chair for the rest of the morning scores of people came in to stare. Civilians of all sorts—old men, young girls—appeared, and gazed as if I were some kind of rare animal in a zoo. Some of the older ones were even sympathetic; and one old lady murmured with tears in her eyes, 'Poveri, poveri, cosi giovane,' and put a piece of bread and some fruit on the floor by the side of my chair. I smiled at her and mumbled my thanks. She was a dear old lady.

During the morning the interpreter came back.

'Your companion has been caught,' he said. 'You see, you can never get away with it. Why try?'

That evening the Capitano from Capua arrived to take me back. He looked at me rather as a father would who has just bailed out his son. 'How could you have let me down like this?' he seemed to say.

'You realize you have committed a grave offence,' he said. 'You will be court-martialled together with Capitano Gilbert, who was re-captured this morning. Your punishment will probably be heavy, as you have caused great distress to the Italian authorities. Such irresponsible conduct is not worthy of an officer.'

With a great show of offended dignity and annoyance he took me to the car. I sat between the Capitano and a subaltern. Behind us sat three soldiers, and facing

41

us were three more. I felt greatly flattered by such a large escort, and, seated thus, we motored the two hundred miles back to Naples.

We reached the city and the big military headquarters there some time in the small hours, and I was put in a cell. There was one blanket, and wrapping this around me, I stretched out on the slatted bed. In spite of the cold, the lack of a pillow and the dreadful hardness of the wooden slats digging into my bones, I was asleep within a few minutes.

I was woken next morning by the rattle of the door being unlocked. To my astonishment and delight, in walked Michael. At the post mortem which followed we tried to work out what had happened on leaving the train, and why we had missed each other immediately after the jump. Michael's actions had been very similar to mine. He had bellowed himself hoarse shouting for me, and had waited about for over an hour. He had come to the conclusion that I had either been hurt and recaptured, or that, for some reason, I hadn't been able to follow him out of the window and was still on the train.

To this day we can neither of us explain why we did not meet as planned. The most likely solution, we decided, was that the train was moving faster than we had thought. If it had been travelling at more than thirty miles an hour, with a gap of five or six seconds between our jumps, we should have been separated by a hundred yards or more, which, at night and in unknown country, can be quite a distance. We had both gone up the mountain-side at right angles to the track; if Michael had scrambled up one re-entrant and I up another, so that a spur of the mountain divided us like a high wall, we shouldn't have heard each other's shouts. This seems the only reasonable explanation of what happened.

Michael, in his usual clear methodical way, had decided to carry on with our original plan of walking the whole distance, moving at night and lying up during the day. Things went reasonably well for the first twenty-four hours, although he found the going terribly slow; but concealment in daylight had proved to be much more difficult than we had imagined. However carefully he chose a hide-out, he was frequently disturbed by peasants coming uncomfortably close; farm workers appeared in the most unlikely places, and even the bleakest and baldest of mountain-sides was never so deserted as it had seemed during the hours of darkness.

Because of this, and the fact that walking at night was proving so incredibly slow, he had abandoned it in favour of travelling openly on roads during the day, and finding a nice comfortable hay-loft at night. This change of plan was his undoing. At a level crossing he was stopped by two Carabinieri and arrested as a suspicious character. If he had looked as haggard as he did when I first set eyes on him that morning, I wonder he wasn't held as a murder suspect!

The Italians quickly realized that they had caught one of the two escaped POWs; and thereafter his experiences had been similar to my own. He was held in a small village police station, fed well and exhibited as a star attraction to the inhabitants for miles around, until he had been collected and brought to join me in Naples.

'Well anyway,' said Michael, 'at least we've learned a lot. We shan't make the same mistakes a second time.'

Later that morning an escort of a captain and four sentries came for us, and we were led off to our Court Martial before General Radice, the general officer commanding the *Carabinieri Reali* in Southern Italy.

8

We were hardly out of our cell when the air raid sirens started to wail, for Flying Fortresses were paying regular visits to Naples at this time. People came swarming out of their offices and raced for the shelters; and in the pandemonium our escort very nearly lost us. However, by dint of much shouting and brandishing of his pistol, the capitano succeeded in ushering our whole party down the stairs. Down and down we went, until we came to a labyrinth of rooms and offices hundreds of feet below the foundations. Here we were left standing in a long narrow corridor. We are both tall—Michael is six foot four—and we were guarded on either side by sentries whose heads barely reached to our chests. Typists, some of them very young and very pretty, and all very friendly, brushed past us with a quite pointless come-hither look in their eyes.

In due course we were ushered into the presence of General Radice, a remarkably dignified-looking man, tall and distinguished, quite unlike any other Italian we had yet come across. Standing in a corner of the room, handcuffed to an NCO, was our wretched sentry of the train. The poor man was in tears and it

44

was a matter of some doubt at this point as to who was being court-martialled—he or us.

The General asked us if we spoke Italian. We said no.

'French, perhaps?'

'Yes, after a fashion.'

'Good,' said the General, 'then we will conduct affairs in French.' Why he chose to hold the trial in a language that not one of us understood particularly well, when he could quite easily have found an interpreter in English somewhere in the building, was difficult to fathom, but his decision added a certain amount of interest to the proceedings.

It was soon obvious that the main intention was the conviction of the sentry. The General, speaking in slow, grammatically perfect French, asked us how we had escaped from the train. In slow, grammatically imperfect French, we told him that we had jumped out of the window. This answer he dismissed as preposterous. It was quite impossible, he said, for anyone guarded as closely as we were, to have jumped out of the train window unless—and here he looked at the wretched sentry—unless we had bribed this miserable man.

'No, that isn't so. We merely lowered the window and jumped out. The sentry did not see us go.'

'You are trying to shield this poor man,' said the General. 'It is obvious that you seduced him from the path of duty by bribery and corruption. I shall send him to prison for two years for his part in your escape.' Here he turned to the sentry and his escort, spoke rapidly in Italian, his voice rising with anger, and ended by dramatically pointing to the door. The sentry, almost collapsing with misery and despair, was literally dragged out of the room, and his wailing cries could be heard diminishing down the corridor.

Then, turning to Michael and me, the General pronounced sentence.

'By the Geneva Convention I have authority to sentence you to thirty days' solitary confinement. It is a great misfortune that I am unable to increase your punishment. People such as you cause untold trouble to the Italian Authorities by your thoughtless and irresponsible action.' He signed to the escort to take us away, and we were led out of the room feeling faintly sorry for the sentry and vaguely pleased with ourselves for getting off so lightly.

The capitano, accompanied by a subaltern and six sentries, drove us back to the camp at Capua from which we had departed only a few days before.

We were given a terrific welcome, and in the evening celebrated in the old fashion. The following morning Michael and I were told that we were to be moved to Chieti that evening. The subaltern who had commanded the guard on the previous journey had been detailed to take us. This duty, which he obviously looked upon with much distaste, was part of his punishment for having allowed us to get away. In addition, he told us, he had been confined to his quarters for a month, and we were left in no doubt as to his opinion of us. He was an extraordinary little fellow, quite good-looking in an oily way. He was evidently petrified that we might escape a second time; but as our journey wore on, however, he relaxed a little, and eventually became so talkative that we found it wearisome.

Could we, he said, be really good fellows and give our parole not to escape on this trip?

'You see,' he said, 'it would make the journey so much

more comfortable for all concerned. We could all go peacefully to sleep and not have to break our backs sitting up all night.'

Michael and I had no intention of sitting up all night; equally we had no intention of making a further futile, and probably suicidal, attempt to jump the train again on this journey. But we said we could not dream of giving our parole. Given the opportunity, we should most certainly be away again. Then we stretched out as comfortably as possible and composed ourselves for sleep.

Sleep was not easy, however, since the lieutenant kept himself, his sentries and us awake by singing at the top of his voice. His repertoire ranged from Grand Opera to Bing Crosby, and I don't think he paused for more than a few minutes from the time the train left Caserta about ten o'clock that night until we steamed into Pescara at seven o'clock the following morning.

The ten-mile trip on to Chieti took a very short time; and about ten o'clock that morning we were marched up to Campo P.G.21. This was situated on the main Rome-Pescara road, of Mille Miglia motor race fame, and lay in a wide valley surrounded by mountains. The town of Chieti, high up on the hillside, looked down into the camp; and in the distance, twenty miles away, the snow-capped Gran Sasso range towered over all. Coloured farm houses dotted the area, and the fields were thick with produce. In such a superb setting, Campo P.G.21, barren and blighted, was a depressing sight.

With an almost audible sigh of relief our escort handed us over to the camp authorities. Three thickly wired and guarded gates clanged behind us; and we were inmates of this bleak place.

It consisted of a series of one-storey buildings arranged in rows on either side of a large dusty expanse. This central area had once been a pleasant field of grass, but countless feet at exercise had ground any life out of it, and the slightest breath of wind caused the dust to rise in choking clouds. The whole establishment was surrounded by a fifteen foot wall, and sentries equipped with searchlights and machine-guns stood guard on platforms at the four corners and half-way along each side. In this way the whole area was thoroughly covered. At the foot of the wall, both inside and out, was a dense entanglement of barbed wire. Some ten yards inside this was a single strand of wire at waist height. This trip wire was liberally posted with notices warning prisoners that anyone crossing it was liable to be shot on sight. One of them stated: 'Passage and Demurrage not allowed on penalty of shooting'. This had many people foxed until, on consulting the dictionary, they found that 'demurrage' was a technical term concerned with the length of time that a railway goods wagon is left lying idle. Obviously the Italians had connected it with the word 'demur', meaning to hesitate, and hence used it to mean 'loitering'.

Michael and I were marched into a hut which was a small prison on its own, complete with its own barbed wire fence which isolated it from the remainder of the camp. Here we were meticulously searched by several repulsive individuals, and I lost some of my money and a compass which, hitherto, I had managed to keep secret.

This undignified procedure was watched throughout by the Commandant, the adjutant and the camp security officer. As each item was discovered and promptly confiscated, their expressions of cynical dis-

approval increased—and so did our indignation. There
was a vindictiveness about the whole thing that got our
goat. I was arguing heatedly with one wretched creature
who insisted on removing a photograph of one of my
girl friends when, suddenly, I lost my temper and
swore at him.

I was immediately set upon by two of the sentries
and knocked to the ground. Michael was similarly
pinioned. Then at the point of a bayonet, and still
cursing and shouting defiance, we were shoved into a
bare room and the door locked behind us. We continued to hurl abuse at them in the same rather childish
fashion, long after they had gone away. The cause of
our outburst was really no more than outraged dignity,
but I felt much better for letting off steam.

A little later, a rather elderly sergeant-major of
Carabinieri entered the room. He explained that he
was our guard, and our sentence started from that
moment. But as there were only three cells in the
punishment block, and the other two were already
occupied, we would be serving our thirty days' solitary
confinement together in the one remaining cell.

We accepted the information philosophically—there
was nothing else we could do—and we felt thankful
that the monotony of solitary confinement would be
tempered by each other's company. We at least had
someone to talk to.

The cell was a large stone-floored room about fifteen
feet square. The window was covered with a wooden
lattice so arranged that light could come in but we
could not look out. The door had a slit like a letter-box
let into it, through which the sentry on guard would,
from time to time, peer with a beady eye. There were
two wooden slatted beds, mattresses, blankets and a

table, and that was all. It was very cold; and, as we looked at it, the room seemed to shrink around us. We were, as you might say, prisoners squared.

Our life in the cell was not unpleasant. Indeed, in retrospect, it was probably the least irksome period of our entire time as prisoners. For one thing, we had a modicum of privacy—and lack of privacy is one of the most irritating aspects of a prisoner's life. For thirty blessed days we were separated from our fellow men. We had plenty of books, sent in by our colleagues outside; and the British camp quartermaster and the OR orderlies saw to it that we were supplied with food and cigarettes. We also received Red Cross food parcels; and for the first time since my original capture I ceased to feel perpetually hungry. In a paradoxical way, we were living in luxury.

We ate, we slept and we read. We had long discussions on abstract subjects, on higher mathematical problems, Rugby football and women, and we spent two hours every day with an Italian grammar and the daily newspaper, improving our Italian. Our jailor, the old Carabinieri, was very helpful over pronunciation, and we co-opted him into hearing us as we read passages aloud from the newspaper. Under his tuition our accents improved and within a very short time we began to speak colloquial Italian of the Abruzzi. We became quite fond of the old boy. He regarded us as naughty children, but he did everything he could to make life pleasant for us and was genuinely sorry that he was unable to do more. We would spend much of our time taking the mickey out of him, a pastime all the more amusing because he rose to the bait so well.

We learnt by heart a particularly bombastic speech of Mussolini's—an oration at the 20th Anniversary celebrations of the *Regia Aeronautica*—and every time the old man entered the cell, jingling his keys in his hand, we would stand and solemnly harangue him with the Duce's words. He took it in very good part, though he was obviously puzzled that we should find amusement in spouting this rot at him; but when we implied that as a good Fascist he should be greatly honoured at hearing the Master's words so often, he showed some annoyance, and said that the Carabinieri were a non-political body, whose allegiance was to their king and not to a pompous fool of a dictator. This reaction surprised us. It was the first evidence we had had of the intense anti-fascist feeling among certain sections of the population.

At exercise time we were able to have a few hurried words with the other two prisoners in the cells. We were marched up and down the one hundred yard strip of concrete path, Mike and I on one path and the other two on a similar strip running parallel with ours. We were not allowed to walk together in the same direction, but for the few seconds as we approached and passed one another on each stretch we managed to snatch a few words.

One of them was the biggest man I had ever seen. His name was Tony Roncoroni, and he had been capped many times as an English second row forward. The last time I had seen him was on a dull February day in 1934, his jersey covered in sweat and Twickenham mud. Peter Glenn, who was with him, was a young American who had volunteered for service with the British Army before America entered the war, and had rendered excellent service in the desert with a Friends' ambulance unit. He had been captured at Alamein. These two had tried to escape by crawling through the fifty feet of wire up to the main gate. They had been spotted while they were still struggling in the wire entanglement; but luckily for them, the sentry had become so excited that he had been unable to shoot straight, and had expended his magazine into the ground all around them. 'The Ronc' and Peter Glenn owed their lives to the fact that, in the pause that followed, the guard had turned out and surrounded them before the sentry could reload and fire again. We missed their company on our exercise walks when, after a week, they finished their thirty days' sentence and were returned to the main camp.

Our days passed easily enough; but by the evening we were bored stiff and looked for ways of passing the time. The most entertaining was 'sentry-baiting'.

At the end of the day, the sentry, left alone to guard what he imagined to be two highly dangerous madmen, became more and more apprehensive. He would peer in every so often, as if expecting to see something dreadful happening inside. If we went on jeering and banging on the door for long enough, he would eventually lose his temper and drive us away from the slit by poking his bayonet through. Then we would grab anything handy and jab it on the end, so that when he pulled it back he never knew what he would find—matchboxes, tins or rotten fruit. It was one way of clearing the cell of garbage, while the little man screamed with rage outside. After a few nights of this, however, the sentries ceased to co-operate and we had to think up a new line.

We began by singing and shouting and banging bed boards against the wall; this softened the sentry up and quickly induced a state of great nervous tension. I would then stand against the wall by the door where he could not see me, while Michael took a bed board and a mattress, and arranged himself so that the Italian could see his head and shoulders. Michael then raised his arm and brought the board down with a resounding thwack on to the mattress, while I let out a shriek of anguish. We kept it up, Mike hitting the mattress with abandoned frenzy and my cries subsiding gradually to a pitiful groan, until we heard the sentry gallop down the corridor to the guardroom, shouting for help at the top of his voice. Immediately, we cleared away the evidence and got into our beds, so that when the sentry returned with the orderly officer and the rest of the guard, we were quietly reading.

The door burst open. We turned with a look of pained surprise at such an untimely intrusion. The orderly officer stood there, pistol in hand. There was silence for a few seconds and then he turned to the sentry.

'You idiot,' he shouted, 'you call me out to say that one prisoner is murdering the other and I find them quietly in bed. You're off your head—imbecile!' Then, to the sergeant of the guard, 'Take him off to the medical officer and lock him up.'

Diversions of this kind helped to relieve the boredom, but even so, time dragged. It says much for us that during the whole thirty days Michael and I never had a serious argument. We knew each other remarkably well, and being in many ways completely opposite characters, we were well suited to endure confinement together. This notorious wrecker of friendships had no effect on ours.

One day I began to itch. At first it was only on my legs, but soon I was scratching my whole body; and on examination I found my skin covered with hundreds of tiny red spots. Scratching merely relieved matters temporarily; afterwards the itching returned with redoubled intensity so that it was impossible to keep still for more than a moment or so. I could not think what caused the trouble.

'Maybe it's lice,' said Michael, 'you'd better have a look.' By this time he too was scratching in a mild, thoughtful way. So we both sat down and examined our clothing. Never have I been more horrified than when I saw the first white body with the red streak down its back and the legs sticking out like oars from a boat. We spent the rest of the day picking over our persons, clothing and blankets, and removed over 150 of the vermin and countless eggs. We shouted and raved at the Carabinieri until the medical officer was sent to us. This gentleman showed little interest.

'It is nothing to worry about,' he said, shrugging his shoulders, 'the entire Italian army is lousy.' He refused to let us have a bath or disinfect our clothing, so that for the rest of our stay in the cell we had the lice with us; and only by the expenditure of a vast amount of time and industry did we manage to keep their numbers in check. We soon got used to it; but I still shudder at the memory of finding those first lice in the seams of my shirt.

On about the twenty-fifth day of our confinement, there were sounds of activity outside, and much coming and going in the Italian Commandant's offices. Our jailer told us that an official of the Swiss Government, as protecting power, was making a visit to the camp to report on conditions to the International Red Cross, and to ensure that the requirements of the Geneva Convention were being met. Naturally the Commandant wished to present his camp in as favourable a light as possible. The good things, the amenities, were highlighted, and the disagreeable side hushed up; and it was therefore inconceivable that any mention of solitary confinement or punishment of any sort would be brought to the visiting official's notice. But one thing was certain. The entourage, on its way from the Italian quarters to the main camp, would have to pass the door of our cell, and, if we had anything to do with it, that Swiss official was going to pay us a visit.

Accordingly, as the tour of inspection reached the corridor, we left our beds and books and started a right old clamour. Frantically the sentry signalled to us to be quiet. Our shouts grew louder, until just as the procession was abreast of our cell, we produced our *pièce de résistance*. Scrabbling wildly at the door, we croaked, '*Acqua—acqua*—for the love of God a little water!' The Swiss appeared not to have heard, but the others had, and it was wonderful to see the look of consternation that crossed the Commandant's face as he quickly hustled the inspector past and out of hearing.

9

On the morning of the thirtieth day our jailer escorted us to the gate into the main camp, and there, with a final admonition to be good in future, he left us. Now, for the first time, we met men who had been in prison for over a year, some even longer, and we were faintly surprised to find them as normal as anyone else. A little quieter and thinner, perhaps, but their mental outlook was sane enough.

Among them were many we knew, old school friends, some of them, and others with whom we had been through OCTU three years before. The older hands were wonderfully generous and helpful. Our clothing was almost beyond repair and we were soon fitted out with shirts and shorts given us by people who had received clothing parcels from home. As always, when new arrivals appeared on the scene, we were questioned at length about news, conditions outside the camp, and any rumours or information we had picked up on the way. This was followed by an official interrogation by the camp escape committee. We told them all we could about the civilian attitude to the war, travelling conditions, guarding of bridges and railways, and a lot of other details they considered relevant. Later we described our actual escape to about three hundred of the inmates of the camp. The meeting assembled ostensibly to listen to a lecture on 'The Principles of Marine Insurance'. The sudden enthusiasm for such a highly specialized subject appeared to arouse no suspicion, and Michael and I told our story to a packed house.

This introduction to the escapist element in the camp was fortunate for us, because immediately afterwards we were approached by various people and invited to join their projects. Normally a newcomer had considerable difficulty in gate-crashing on a tunnel or some other scheme, and had to wait weeks or even months before he could get a foot in the door. But our experience of conditions outside was considerably greater than anyone else's, and so our advice was much sought after.

There were no less than four tunnels in progress at

that moment. Italian security guards were extremely active, and the 'Ferrets', carabinieri working in pairs, spent the entire day inside the compound, searching every inch of ground and building for signs of tunnelling activity. Quite a number of projects which had been progressing well, sometimes for months, had been sprung through some slight slip-up, or because of inadequate security arrangements, and the ferrets would stand in triumph while the workings were dug up and filled in.

After each fresh tunnel was found there would be a systematic search of the entire camp. These snap searches were a danger as well as a nuisance, since one rarely got more than two or three minutes' warning. A group of prisoners standing in the compound would see an ominous muster of sentries forming up ready to march in. There would be a hasty cry of 'Search! Search!' yelled into each hut, whereupon one would frantically hide any tools or other valuable items of kit that were lying about; sentries would surround the huts, which were cleared, and the prisoners would assemble in the middle of the compound. Then there was a roll-call. How long one was kept out in the compound depended on the intensity of the search; it could be two hours; on one memorable occasion it was sixteen hours. This was after it was discovered that a hammer, belonging to an Italian workman who had come in to do a little plumbing, had been stolen. Good tunnelling tools were at a premium, and no opportunity of appropriating such valuables as hammers, chisels or indeed any blunt instrument, was ever missed. When the theft was discovered, the repercussions were fast and furious. It was the culmination of a series of such thefts in a very few weeks, and in spite of searches not one of the tools had been recovered. This final act of lawlessness was too much for the Commandant; by hook or by crook he was going to have that hammer back, if it meant ransacking the huts, tearing down walls and ripping up bedding. But when at the end of the day the sentries were called off, tired, hungry and dispirited, they were still minus the hammer.

The following morning a muster parade was called. The entire camp was lined up in fives in the courtyard. The Commandant, who seldom put in an appearance inside the compound, marched on to the parade. A box was placed on the ground, and, standing on it, he addressed us thus.

'A hammer has been stolen from a civilian workman.' Cheers from the assembled prisoners.

'I am determined to recover this hammer.' More cheers from the prisoners.

'I shall recover this hammer if I have to keep you standing out here day and night for a week.' Boos from the prisoners.

'I therefore give you a chance to avoid this unpleasantness. Will the man who stole the hammer step forward.' Silence from the prisoners.

'For the last time—where is the hammer?' Silence for a few seconds, and then a small officer in the front rank took a pace forward and very solemnly said: 'Sir, I stole the hammer and put it down the well.'

The well was in the middle of the compound. It was full of water and apparently bottomless. Any normal person would have realized he was having the mickey taken out of him. Not so the Commandant. With a wave of his arms he dismissed the parade. Orders were shouted to the adjutant, who doubled smartly away to the offices. Within minutes the Chieti fire engine could be heard thundering down the road from the town. Gates were flung open, and to the accompaniment of rousing cheers from us all the engine roared into the compound, its bell jangling and firemen clinging all over it. Immediately they started to pump the well dry.

This was really too good to be true. A cheering mob of prisoners whooped round and round the engine; bagpipes skirled, instruments of all descriptions added to the din and a scene of the utmost pandemonium reigned. Within seconds the hose had been hacked in several places by razor blades and penknives. Spouts of water shot in all directions until the suction was so reduced that a mere trickle issued from the nozzle. After some minutes of this unequal struggle the Italians gave in. After salvaging what they could of their ruined hose, they remounted the engine and drove away. Some minutes later, when the noise had begun to subside and the prisoners were still wiping the tears of laughter from their eyes, there was a great shout from the main gate. The leading fireman was standing there, waving his arms hysterically and screaming with rage. Someone had stolen the fire engine's tool-box!

In spite of the undoubted misery and wretchedness of our situation, we still managed to see the lighter side of life; and in retrospect it seems to me that I had as much fun then as at any time before or since. The Italians made perfect stooges, and, since we had no responsibilities, we exploited every possibility. It wasn't all fun but the comradeship of some magnificent men in adversity was an experience that I would be very sorry to have missed.

Our stay at Chieti main camp was short. Five days after leaving the cooler Mike and I were moved. The trouble-makers, the escapers and other fractious elements, dubbed by the Italian officials as '*Molto Pericoloso*', were removed en bloc to a new camp in the north of Italy. Accompanied as usual by numerous sentries, we entrained at Chieti and left Campo P.G.21 behind us. I was not sorry; the place was a depressing dump and its air of frustration and decay would quickly have got on my nerves.

The journey was marred by one unfortunate incident. A young RAF officer—he was not yet twenty-one—had told his friends in camp that he would get away on this journey if it killed him. He had worked himself up into such a state of tension that on two occasions his companions had forcibly restrained him from making what would have been a suicidal jump; but then, when the others thought he had calmed down, he gave them the slip.

The train was crawling through a small station. It was broad daylight and the sentries were very much on the alert. Suddenly, he dived out of the window and ran along the platform. The guard in the corridor fired and brought him down. Immediately afterwards there was a ragged volley, and every sentry on the train, which had stopped, fired at the man as he lay wounded on the platform. Then there was a pause, and for several seconds it was so quiet you could have heard a pin drop. The sentries, white-faced and terrified, stood over us with their fingers on their triggers. One incautious move and there would have been a massacre.

The NCO boarded the train again. He came down the corridor, paused, genuflected and said, 'Your young friend is dead.'

For the remainder of our journey north the tension and the quiet were uncanny. No outbursts greeted the inhuman behaviour of the sentries, and our very calmness seemed to make them more frightened and nervous. When we eventually reached the end of the trip they were in a state bordering on complete exhaustion.

We could not see much of the camp itself since it was pitch dark and pouring with rain when we arrived, but a reception committee from the few prisoners already there gave us a great welcome. The internal organization was excellent, and for the first time in my captivity I was greeted with a hot meal, on, of all luxuries, clean china plates. There was no overcrowding and none of the usual squalid atmosphere. That night I slept in a comfortable sprung bed with a hair mattress in surroundings more pleasant than anything I had experienced since leaving England.

Campo P.G.49 was situated in the middle of Fontanellato—a small village some five miles north of Parma in the Po valley—and consisted of a single modern building which had formerly been an orphanage, built by the church.

It consisted of three floors and a basement, and had two wings, one on each side of a central hall. This hall had stained glass windows, and an intricate mosaic floor. A gallery extended round three of the walls at the level of the first floor; it was probably the former chapel. There were dormitories on all three floors with from six to twenty beds according to the size of the room. The beds were single spring cots, and each had a small cupboard alongside it for toilet kit. There were wash basins and lavatories on each floor and shower baths in the basement. Also in the basement were the parcel and quartermaster's stores and the Mess-room.

All this was in striking contrast to the squalor and

overcrowding of the wretched Chieti camp, with its two thousand inhabitants. Here there were only four hundred of us all told. A messing committee arranged menus and augmented the Italian rations with Red Cross food; no parcels were issued to individuals, but everything was handed in bulk to the kitchens. As a result, the food was excellent, well-cooked, and served in a civilized manner, and one did not need to keep half-eaten tins of food in one's locker. I personally found this one of the most admirable aspects of the new camp; and, taken with the pleasant surroundings, it acted as balm to one's irritated nerves. One no longer hated one's fellow men merely because one shared a room with them.

On the other hand, the wire fortifications were as impregnable as ever; and the fact that the camp consisted of a single building made tunnelling virtually impossible. The area in front was out of bounds and wired off; there was one main entrance gate through the wire at the end of the building, and the usual four sentry platforms at the four corners of the wire. The one drawback in Campo P.G.49 was the lack of exercise room: all we had was a courtyard, running the length of the orphanage at the back and about twenty yards wide.

In contrast to Chieti, whose internal organization was chaotic, the camp was extremely efficiently run by the Senior British Officer and his staff. When we arrived the SBO was a charming character by the name of Lowsley-Williams, a regular cavalry major who had been captured very early on in the desert campaign. He was scrupulously polite to everyone, and in particular handled the Italians with great delicacy and tact. His diplomacy gained many concessions from them which greatly added to our creature comforts. The adjutant was Dicky Black of the 4th Hussars, well known as a steeplechase jockey.

The high standard of the British command was matched by their Italian counterparts—a notable change from the usual run. The Commandant was just and equable, and gave the impression of being an excellent soldier. He was no fool and had the situation well under control; there were no loopholes. Unlike so many of his brethren, he realized that it was a POW's duty to try and escape, just as it was his duty to try and stop us. Because of his efficiency and fore-sight, he kept the advantage firmly with himself.

The Second-in-Command had for years been the London agent of an Italian business house and had unconsciously adopted many of our ways, including the habit of sucking a pipe. He spoke perfect English and was extremely friendly towards us; at the same time, and despite his obvious dislike of the war, and the misfortune which had put us on opposite sides, he was never heard to utter a single word to the detriment of his own country, its government or its allies. This tendency to knock their own side became increasingly prevalent among certain Italians as Italy's plight went from bad to worse.

The security officer and interpreter was a very different character. His name was Prevedini; he had been on the staff of Cook's before the war, and he had conducted numerous British tourists through Italy. He spoke English fluently with just a trace of a cockney accent; and because of a considerable mastery of our slang, he got on very well with some of our orderlies. He professed to have no love of the Fascist régime, and to live for the day when retribution caught up with

Mussolini. But he was altogether too plausible and genial, and we shunned him like the plague.

The rest of the staff were a nondescript bunch, with little to distinguish them, apart from one small, elderly, irritable red-faced lieutenant, popularly known as 'the Bed-bug'.

Michael and I shared a room with about twenty other officers on the top floor of the building. From the windows there was a magnificent view of the rich farmlands of the Po valley stretching away to the mountains of the Dolomites and Switzerland. We had a number of talented painters in the camp, and they revelled both in this view and in others of the village itself seen from the front of the orphanage. Between them they produced some really good pictures; in particular, Captain John Dugdale's portraits in ink and water-colour were masterly.

The camp abounded with 'characters', from all walks of life, from Yorkshire sheep farmer to Mayfair play-boy. Within a camp of this size one's acquaintances are numerous and one's close friends few, but friendships formed under such conditions usually last a lifetime.

Ours was a high-spirited room. The far end was metaphorically curtained off. Consisting mainly of Guardsmen and Household Cavalry, it was referred to as 'Grosvenor Square'. Officers of the Brigade are a quite definite species. They are beings apart, and their surroundings have not the slightest effect on their behaviour. Whether they are leading an attack at Tobruk, floundering in the mud of Tunis's Longstop Hill, or condemned to the misery of captivity, their conversation seldom turns from London's social round. They might for all the world be dining at the Savoy. To those who do not know them it is a perplexing characteristic, but one that I personally find wholly admirable.

The other end of the room Michael and I shared with Peter Barshall and four others. These four alone make an absorbing study. Ian Frazer was an extremely efficient regular Indian Army captain. He was passionately devoted to his career and would delight us with stories about his Frontier Force riflemen, magnificent hill warriors. At the same time he was the very antithesis of the layman's conception of an Indian Army officer, since he was a Doctor of Philosophy who had taken a double first at Oxford and a miler of the first rank. Of all the prisoners I ever met, Ian was the least perturbed by his situation; he possessed a remarkable tranquillity in the face of misfortune that I found very enviable.

Donald Shaw was a perfect example of a rapidly disappearing breed in England, the yeoman farmer. He had been sent out to Palestine with his regiment, The Cheshire Yeomanry, early in 1940. The Yeomanry Brigade, of which this regiment formed a part, was the sole remaining horsed foundation in the British Army at that time; but, much to everyone's disappointment, the Brigade was broken up in 1941, and the officers and men posted to mechanized units in the Middle East. When he was captured in 1942 Donald was the Brigade Signals Officer of a formation in the Tobruk garrison. Before the war he had been reading medicine at Oxford, but his heart was in the land, and it was his intention to farm after his demobilization. Correct in his behaviour on all occasions, clean-shaven, tall and upright, Donald would have made an ideal head boy at any public school, a position which he did in fact hold at Oundle before going up to Oxford.

Eric Newby had been captured while taking part in a Commando raid on the Sicilian coast. He had paddled ashore with five others in collapsible rubber canoes from a submarine surfaced a few miles off. They carried with them rucksacks filled with explosives and detonators, their objective being a large and important airfield. Unfortunately they were unable to reach it and had had to content themselves with wrecking some electrical installations and pylons. On the return journey to their rendezvous with the submarine, it started to blow, and some miles offshore the canoes capsized. Somehow all of them managed to remain afloat until daylight, when an Italian fishing boat picked them up.

Eric had an irresponsible sense of humour, a delightful and witty personality, and quite the best physique I have seen on any man.

With such companions life was far from dull, although the continual nagging monotony of our loss of freedom was always there. We spent our days lying in the sun, reading, walking, playing interminable rubbers of bridge. A small orchestra was formed, and, under the direction of an American soldier of fortune, 'Admiral' Raeder, concerts were organized. Such diversions were merciful breaks in the boredom of life, and few audiences could have been more appreciative than we were.

A balcony extended along the front of the building at a level of the first floor overlooking the main street of the village. In the evenings, when the air was pleasantly cool after the stifling heat of an Italian summer's day, we would sit there with a mug of vino, yarning and watching the village go by. The girls, all looking ravishing to our starved eyes, paraded up and down the main street with the sole purpose of showing their charms to this captive audience.

Campo P.G.49 had another great advantage. Once a week those who elected to, were allowed, under heavy guard and on parole, to go for a walk. The prisoners would turn out as immaculately dressed as possible, boots shining and uniforms neatly pressed; and, marching in columns of threes, were led by Prevedini for a good two hours' ramble round the countryside. I looked forward to these excursions with great impatience. Apart from our natural enjoyment of the exercise and fresh air, we soon acquired a pretty exact knowledge of the lie of the land for some miles round the camp— a knowledge put to very good use later on.

10

These walks were the only means of keeping ourselves fit during the first few weekes at Fontanellato. The courtyard was so cramped that few people used it for exercise, and for the majority the weekly walks sufficed. A few fitness maniacs, however, needed more than that, and they used to run up and down the three flights of stairs. I tried it myself and can state with certainty that I know of no more fatiguing manner in which to take exercise. But within a few weeks an alternative to this arduous task presented itself. A largish field immediately behind the camp was enclosed with wire and two sentry platforms were erected at the far corners. A gateway, extending the length of the old courtyard, was cut in the wire, and the new exercise compound was opened for our use from 10 a.m. to 5 p.m. At five we had to quit the field, the gateway was closed, and the two sentries on the new platforms were withdrawn.

The field had been a meadow belonging to a nearby farm. Its surface was uneven and sloping and unsuitable for playing any ball games; but when we pointed this out to the Commandant, picks and shovels were produced, and a large party of prisoners set to work to level it. Punctually at five o'clock each evening the tools were collected and counted, and the compound was closed for the night.

It was during this operation that two officers devised a possible method of escape. Their idea was to dig a small trench in the field while the levelling process was going on. On the appointed day they would slip into the trench and be covered over, and the surface would be levelled. Then, after dark, when the two sentries had been withdrawn, they could clamber out of the trench and climb over the unguarded wire at their leisure. It was a brilliantly simple scheme, but it required the assistance of a considerable number of volunteer diggers. If it worked, and the hole was carefully covered by the first two escapees when they left it, then the following night two more might repeat the performance, and so on. The only limitation was the impossibility of keeping the absence of more than six prisoners from the Italians' notice for any length of time.

Considering that the two platform sentries were gazing straight down on to the field of operations, and that another sentry stood with the digging party the whole time, the actual digging of the trench had to be cleverly done. The first steps were reasonably easy; but as soon as the groove became a definite hole and finally a trench, the task of keeping it from the sentries' eyes became exceedingly difficult. It took some days to complete; and at the end of each digging session it had to be roofed in, first with wooden slats, and then with earth arranged on top of them. Moreover, the camouflage had to be good enough to deceive the sentry, who systematically examined the area, armed with a long iron prod, immediately after the field had been cleared at the end of each day.

Another difficulty was that the levelling operation was in danger of being finished before the trench. The Italian authorities had been persuaded against their better judgement to provide the digging implements, and they were extremely anxious to get them all back into safe keeping. So the diggers started to go slow, and whereas the first two-thirds of the field were completed in a week, the last third took nearly a fortnight.

But, at last, the trench was finished, and it only remained to stow the first two escapers, and their kit, in it. This was achieved by the simple expedient of playing a game of rugger on the levelled pitch. To begin with, the sentries were fascinated by the spectacle of thirty men playing such a game at the height of the Italian summer; but after a bit their attention was distracted to other parts of the field. A scrum was conveniently formed over the hole. The scrum collapsed, and when the players slowly and painfully extricated themselves, Lieutenant Day, of the Worcester Regiment, and his companion, were securely buried in their grave and the surface had been smoothed over. Then the game continued.

At five o'clock the field was cleared as usual, and the sentry examined it. He seemed to spend ages on the rugger pitch and appeared to be prodding every square inch. At last, however, he came away satisfied, and a host of dry throats swallowed again.

Roll-call that evening was rigged. Normally one walked in single file from one side of the courtyard to the other and was counted by the Italian Orderly Officer as one passed him. Having counted all those on parade, he then visited the sick-room and counted the invalids. On this occasion, two men, having been counted in the courtyard, slipped past the sentry guarding the door and ran down the corridor to the sick quarters, where they were counted a second time. The Italians discerned nothing wrong and the parade was dismissed.

There was another check during the early hours of the morning when the orderly officer went from room to room counting the sleeping bodies, so two life-size dummies were placed in the sick-room beds. All went according to plan, and Day and his friend had an excellent start with no suspicions aroused. Nothing unusual was heard during the night; and the following morning, when the exercise compound was opened, the hole, neatly covered, was found to be empty.

The second party decided to give the two men forty-eight hours to get clear before they made their attempt. The roll-call procedure was repeated; nothing went amiss; and it seemed that the pair had indeed been handed a flying start. However, there was an inexplicable air of suspicion and tension among the sentries that day, and the second party postponed their attempt for another twenty-four hours. On the following day, that is seventy-two hours after the first two had got away, Tony Roncoroni, Toby Graham and Peter Joscelyn were successfully hidden in the hole. How three grown men—one of them the size of 'The Ronc' —could have got into the hole at all, will always remain a mystery. It seemed a physical impossibility; and yet the three of them remained there, unable to move an inch, not only while the sentry searched the field but during the next seven hours as well.

At midnight a mild diversion was arranged inside the camp. A barrage of shouts and singing ensured that the sentries focused their attention on the building and away from the dark patch of the exercise compound, while the second party climbed out of the hole and over the wire to freedom. Then the singing gradually ceased, and there was no further disturbance.

Soon after breakfast next morning, however, it became obvious that something had gone wrong. The exercise compound was securely shut, and a group of the camp staff stood in the middle of the rugger pitch, busily peering into the hole. There was an immediate roll-call, and each prisoner was counted and his name called. Under this system it was impossible to cover up for the missing men; and by the end of the parade the Italians realized that not one or two, but five men had escaped. We were then treated to the delightful spectacle of five of the guard attempting to pack themselves into the trench, while the Commandant stood imperiously over them. At last they gave up this obviously impossible task; and the staff were forced to admit that the hole had been used more than once. The Commandant stalked off, a very irate man.

Meanwhile we were on tenterhooks. Then just before midday Toby Graham was led into the Italian staff buildings, clad only in his trousers and undervest. Three hours later Tony and 'Joss' also arrived, under heavy escort. By that evening all three were in the cooler, starting their thirty days. There was still no news of the first two.

We were longing to hear what had befallen Tony Roncoroni and company and it was worth waiting for. To begin with things had gone amazingly well. When the sounds of the diversion from inside had reached the three lying in indescribable discomfort in the hole, they had climbed out one at a time, intending to cross the wire at five minute intervals. Tony and Joss made it without any trouble, and duly met at the pre-arranged rendezvous, a tree some two hundred yards north of the compound. They were waiting impatiently for Toby when, from away in the darkness behind them, there came a series of appallingly loud twangs, followed by silence. There was no sign of Toby. Tony and Joss waited for half-an-hour, and then reluctantly left the rendezvous and set out to walk the five miles to Parma station. The train was due soon after 5 a.m. and they were already well behind schedule, so they had to step out.

Their nondescript working men's clothing and cloth hats were a convincing disguise, and they had money and excellent forged papers for their role as Spanish labourers working in Italy. They arrived at the station in time, bought their tickets without trouble, and duly boarded the crowded Milan train on the first leg of their journey to the frontier and Switzerland. On arrival at Milan they intended to change trains and take the Milan–Chiasso express. At Chiasso, the Italian–Swiss border town, Tony Roncoroni had relatives. With their assistance, the last two miles across the frontier into freedom should be reasonably easy.

While Tony and Joss were standing in the crowded

corridor of the Parma–Milan train, Toby Graham was trotting, breathless, through the fields in an effort to reach the station in time. He was, he knew, desperately late. As last man out of the hole, he had carefully replaced the wooden cover and re-arranged the earth then started to wriggle as fast as he could through the wire. He hadn't gone far when his sporting civilian shirt got firmly caught on the barbs. Every time he moved there was a resounding twang. To his tense nerves each sound seemed to echo in the still night air. For minutes at a time he lay still before trying once again to extricate himself; but the more he struggled the faster he was held. The whole wire seemed to jangle with his movements, and at any moment he expected the dread searchlight to swing round and pick him out in its beam. At last, with a final frenzied effort, he succeeded in hauling himself clear, but in so doing, he left the tattered remnants of his shirt behind.

By now he was nearly an hour adrift. With reckless haste he scrambled across fields and through ditches, but when he reached the station, dishevelled and drenched in sweat, it was to discover that the train had gone. Wearing only an undervest and trousers, he was somewhat conspicuous, even in war-time Italy. The station Carabinieri, who had so recently examined and passed the papers of Tony Ronc and Joss, eyed Toby with suspicion. Toby's Italian was negligible and his Spanish no better, and when the Carabinieri looked at his papers, they immediately smelt a rat. Toby was held for further interrogation, and urgent telephone calls were made. The train was stopped, and the two 'Spanish workmen' were duly arrested. One more stop and they would have been in Milan.

And so another magnificently thought-out scheme

had gone astray, foundering on a trivial detail which not even the most careful planning could have avoided.

Nothing was heard of Day and his companion for nearly four weeks. Just when it was generally thought that they must have successfully crossed the frontier into Switzerland, they were brought back, thin and bearded and blackened by the sun, under heavy guard to the camp. They had almost made it. The four days' grace before their escape was discovered had enabled them to get well clear of the area by the time the Italians put out their drag-net and cordoned off the surrounding countryside. They had walked, avoiding roads and large villages, living mainly on vegetables and fruit gathered on the journey. They had traversed the Po valley, crossing the river by stealing a fisherman's boat, and had reached the Swiss frontier near Como. They were actually reconnoitering the best way across the frontier defences when they had run into a patrol, and were arrested before they could turn round. They could see the inhabitants of the Swiss village just over the border quite plainly.

In glorious summer weather the days dragged slowly by. The exercise compound was a boon. Eight-a-side teams were formed and a Rugby knock-out competition organized. We played twenty minutes each way under the broiling sun and in a dense dust cloud; but in spite of the heat and the hardness of the ground, very few people got hurt. These games were a source of great enjoyment to players and spectators alike, among the latter most of the village population, who would gaze with awe and a good deal of amusement at the heroic battles being fought within the wire cage. From our point of view, it passed the time and kept us fit. In any case there was nothing else to do.

The morale of the camp was exceptionally high. Every day the Italian radio and newspapers spoke of fresh reverses and disasters. The Axis were cleared out of Africa and the invasion of Sicily was well under way. Even the most ardent pessimist felt that Italy's days in the war were numbered, and that an invasion of the Italian mainland would bring about the collapse of the Fascist régime. Even so, various schemes for a break-out were in hand. Tunnelling was well nigh impossible. Any tunnel had to start from the basement of the one building; but the basement was terribly easy to search, and Prevedini and his two ferrets paid it daily visits, tapping each brick and prodding each crevice and floor tile. The Guards had started one project there, but it had been discovered within a week. The Italians reacted quickly and drastically. They dug a trench about ten feet deep right round the camp. It was impossible to tunnel under it since at this depth they had reached the water level. At a stroke, therefore, they completely wiped out digging as a means of escape.

However, with the war going so well for the Allies, we had a more urgent preoccupation. If and when the Italians dropped out, there was a strong possibility that we might all be transported to Germany. We knew, moreover, that it would be done quickly and efficiently, with no warning at all; and so Michael and I worked out a plan of action—just in case.

We decided to build a hide in the camp to which we could scuttle if the Germans took the place over, and where we could stay until it was empty. The basement was hopeless, because Prevedini still searched it regularly in spite of the moat-trench; but we discovered an interesting possibility. A flight of stone steps led up to the original entrance of the orphanage. The surveyors in the camp told us that these steps were in all probability built on a framework of concrete pillars leaving a fairish cavity underneath. Here was the ideal hide-out, but the entrance to it was a difficult problem. We finally chose a spot in the corner of one of the ground floor rooms; Prevedini only looked for tunnels in the basement. We lifted nine floor tiles and set them into a wooden tray to make a trap door. This could be removed bodily while we were digging, and then put back at the end of the session. Except on the most minute inspection, the floor appeared unblemished.

Our intention was to dig down about two feet, and then strike diagonally through the outside wall into the cavity under the stone steps. It was appallingly hard work; the floor was concrete, and after chipping away at it for days with an improvised chisel and hammer, our progress was measured in inches. But, reinforced by four new members of the project, including Toby Graham and Eric Newby, we gradually extended our excavation to a foot and then to eighteen inches. After a month we had made a hole under our tile trap door that was big enough for that purpose, and had started to attack the wall itself.

It was about this time that the most momentous news broke on the camp. On 21 July, at about 9 p.m., a great commotion was heard from the Italian quarters. There were sounds of cheering and singing; and quickly an excited and happy crowd of villagers gathered in the road outside. The SBO called a muster parade in the central hall. When all were assembled, he said:

'Gentlemen, the Commandant has just informed me that Mussolini has been deposed. The Fascist régime in Italy has ended.'

The news knocked us sideways. The optimists expected the Italians to sign an armistice immediately, and we all thought that things would move rather faster than in fact they did. For the first few days our excitement and exhilaration were intense. All Fascist posters were torn down with much bravura by the Italian troops; the ridiculous slogans were painted out from walls and buildings; and busts of Mussolini were publicly broken. On our walks we were greeted with friendly enthusiasm and many cries of '*Viva gli Inglesi*'. But—and a big BUT it was— we were still prisoners of war; and as our first high hopes of early freedom faded, an acute feeling of anticlimax settled on the camp, which was worse in many ways than the usual run of boredom and frustration. After only three days of resting from our labours, we started digging once more. While hoping for the best, we prepared for the worst.

The Senior British Officer, Lt-Col De Burgh, had built up a highly efficient organization which not merely ran the camp, but also formed a well-disciplined force capable of dealing with any treachery on the part of the Italians. We were split up into five companies, each approximately one hundred strong and each having a commander and an adjutant. For the two daily roll-calls, which were SBO's parades, the camp formed up in companies. This made counting easier and saved a great deal of time.

Although during the weeks immediately following the Mussolini débacle no cloud in the form of German troops marred the serenity of our horizon, the SBO very wisely prepared against any eventuality. His orders from the War Office were to keep the camp together as an integrated unit during the period between the signing of an armistice and the arrival of Allied troops in the area. The Allied Occupation forces would want to avoid, if possible, small groups of ex-POWs wandering independently about the countryside and making their own way home, as it were, and thus complicating the job of screening and looking after the many thousands of men awaiting repatriation. The orders were clear but not stringent, and the SBO was at liberty to modify them at his discretion, if the situation so dictated.

The month of August was uncannily peaceful. The campaign in Sicily had ended and everyone awaited daily the news that the invasion of Italy had begun. There was no sign of any German activity in the neighbourhood, and, according to Prevedini and the Second-in-Command, not much German traffic on the roads.

For ever optimistic, the consensus at this time was that the Germans would make no attempt to hold Southern and Central Italy, but would rapidly withdraw to the line of the Po, or even to the Austrian frontier. Examined in the cold light of logic this was a ridiculous hypothesis, since, even discounting the Germans' natural vindictiveness at what they were bound to consider an act of treachery on the part of their ally, Italy presented the most perfect defensive country in Europe. By holding it the Germans not only contained a large Allied force whose added weight would have been welcome on the other fronts, but also helped themselves liberally to the ample produce of the fertile north of Italy. However, prisoners are not logical people, and the thought that the Nazis would do anything but make a very rapid—albeit fighting—withdrawal never entered our minds. What did enter our minds, however, was the probability that in the course of this retreat the Boche would grab all the prisoners he could. The fact that our camp was so far north did not make us any happier; and the tension mounted almost to breaking point during the last days of August.

When the 8th Army crossed the Straits of Messina and landed in Calabria, it was obvious that the Italian armistice was imminent. The Commandant and Col De Burgh conferred on the situation. The SBO reminded him that in the event of a cessation of hostilities between Great Britain and Italy it was the Commandant's duty to ensure that we were safely handed over to the British authorities, and that he must defend the camp against possible German intervention, and afford us every assistance within his power. The Commandant agreed to these points, adding that, as soon as he received official information that an armistice had been signed, a gap would be cut in the wire at the rear of the camp

The SBO called a muster parade.

'Gentlemen,' he said, 'you are all perfectly aware of the risk of a German attack on this camp. The Italians state—for what it is worth—that if necessary they will fight to defend us, but it is quite obvious that a determined German attack, however small, would be bound to succeed eventually. In the light of these circumstances I have instituted these orders. At the first sign of an approaching German formation, the general alarm will be sounded by the bugler. The camp will then muster in the compound by companies, and we will march out in good order and with military discipline to an area which my representative is at this moment reconnoitering with the Italian Second-in-Command. I believe the Italians will act in good faith and I do not think there will be treachery.'

We had continued to work on our hide-out until the SBO told us of the arrangements he had made for the security of the camp; after that we reckoned it was redundant. We never did get through the wall. A pity, in a way, as I felt sure it was the digging project '*par excellence*', and that it would have defied the most intensive search.

On the morning of 9 September we awoke to see a group of Italians removing the wire at the far end of the exercise compound. Others were engaged in digging weapon pits round the perimeter. They were not unduly agitated, so we knew at once that no German attack was imminent. Few of us had any illusions about the amount of fighting they would do, but the gap in the wire was a comforting sight. The excitement was intense; and although there had been no official information of an armistice, rumours of one were rife.

Michael had been in the sick quarters for the previous three weeks with a carbuncle the size of a man's fist in his left armpit. On this particular morning he had only been out of bed one day, and was feeling pretty groggy. I was sitting with him in the sick bay, helping to organize his small kit, when the three G's were sounded. This particular bugle call gives a sense of extreme urgency at any time; on this occasion it was positively imperative. Within minutes the camp was assembled in the courtyard. Then quietly, and in an orderly manner, we marched out through the gap in the wire. The only man in the sick bay who was unable to walk was Eric Newby, who had broken his ankle ten days previously. For him the Italians produced a horse, a sad-looking animal, only just up to Eric's weight. With an Italian holding the beast's head Eric rode in the van while behind him, the rest of us, marching in companies, quickly moved out of the camp.

PART TWO

The Long Walk South

I

We had seen the guards drop their weapons and run,
and the villagers scuttle off into their houses and bar
and bolt their doors, and from the panic, it was obvious
that the Germans were not far away. The villagers
were under no illusions as to what the German mood
would be when they discovered that the birds had
flown, and so, very wisely, they were keeping out of
sight.

I felt very much happier once we had put a good
quarter-of-an-hour's march between ourselves and the
village. My sense of security increased as we penetrated
deeper into the maze of rich cultivated farmland with
its olive groves and cypresses.

After some forty minutes' marching the column
halted and dispersed in a grove of small stunted trees.
Companies were well separated, and the whole 'laager'
area covered about a half-mile square. Through the
middle ran a dry river bed, perhaps twenty feet wide
and fifteen feet deep, and dotted with bushes. Here the
SBO set up his headquarters. Orders were issued to
companies to remain as quiet and still as possible, and

to be prepared to stay put until after dark. Meanwhile, Capt Stewart Hood, a fluent Italian linguist, set out with the Italian Second-in-Command to return to the village and find out how things stood. On the way back they put on civilian clothes, borrowed from a farmer, in order to avert suspicion.

It was about noon when Stewart Hood departed, and I remember the intense heat of the shimmering atmosphere, as Mike and I lay in the olive grove reading the *Corriere della Sera* of that fateful day. Blazoned across the front page in four-inch black lettering was the one word '*Armistizio*'. It was followed by a brief communiqué from General Badoglio, stating that an armistice had been signed with the Allied powers. In view of the military situation now pertaining, the overwhelming power of the Allied armies, and in order to avoid further useless bloodshed and destruction of Italian cities, he, Marshal Badoglio, had surrendered unconditionally the Army, Navy and Air Force of His Majesty King Emanuel VI. The war was now over. There was not one word about German reaction to this volte face, and no hint of the intentions of the German military fighting in Italy at that time. As a source of information the paper was useless to us, but the satisfaction of reading about our enemy's surrender in one of his own great newspapers was an experience not to be missed.

Speculation as to our own situation was as optimistic as ever. We had no doubt that the Germans were even now evacuating the country as fast as they could, and that British troops would reach us in a matter of days. The strategists pointed out the absolute certainty of landings from the sea around Genoa and Ancona, in order to bag as much of the German force as possible. All were agreed that the river line of the Po was the only position the Germans could hope to hold for any length of time; and since we were south of it, we were sitting pretty.

About three o'clock that afternoon the Second-in-Command and Stewart Hood returned. Apparently four lorry loads of German troops had arrived about five minutes after we had left, and there had been much consternation and rage when they found the camp empty. They had ransacked the building in typical German fashion, taking away what kit they could and destroying the rest. There had been some firing, but no casualties. Then taking the Commandant with them as a prisoner, they had left as abruptly as they arrived. Just before our informants had set off back, a motor-cycle patrol had driven through the village, so it was not considered safe to return.

On hearing this the SBO called the company commanders together and told them that, in his opinion, the best thing to do was for us to remain where we were as an integrated unit, until the situation became clearer. So, after dark, the outlying companies would close on the river bed and spend the night there; sentries would be posted, and a listening post established on the road which ran past about four hundred yards away.

During the rest of that day nothing disturbed our peace and quiet, and so, at about nine o'clock in the evening we moved across to the line of the river. The night was beautifully clear and warm, and a great-coat was all the covering we needed. Those not on sentry go were soon sleeping soundly. Michael and I were on duty from 2 a.m. to 4 a.m., and although it was rather chillier by this time, the atmosphere was delightfully clear and fresh, and the feeling of freedom was intoxicating. Lying there, peering over the darkened fields, we could hear the dull thud of explosions in the distance, and flashes lit up the night sky for seconds on end. In the direction of the main road, the Via Emilia from Rimini to Milan, there were sounds of much traffic; and this tied in neatly with our pre-conceived ideas of German intentions. Explosions, we said, meant the destruction of dumps prior to a hasty withdrawal, and the sound of traffic was the sound of the withdrawal itself. The possibility that the flow of traffic was moving south instead of north never occurred to us. Comforted by our satisfactory deductions, we passed the night cheerfully, discussing the parties we should have when we returned to the regiment.

Shortly after dawn the following morning the first of an amazing cavalcade of farmers and peasants began arriving. Carrying gifts of food and clothing, these charming people showered us with friendliness—and a veritable cornucopia of false information. Preferring not to be the bearers of bad tidings, they tailored the news to suit the occasion; and if good news would cheer us up then good news they would bring. By midday there were so many reports, from those who had listened to the BBC news service with their own ears, that we were quite convinced that Allied landings had occurred all along the Adriatic coast, that a British force was advancing unopposed to the north, and that the Germans were in full flight. However, the SBO was sceptical and sent an officer to a neighbouring farm to listen to the BBC news and report back. This sensible precaution probably saved us all from disaster.

During the rest of that day, in spite of the over-optimistic rumours emanating from the Italian civilians, it gradually became apparent that things were not going quite as well as we had hoped. There were reports of fighting between the German and Italian garrisons in Milan and Rome, and also in Parma, only five miles away. Here the Germans had used tanks, had occupied the place after a fight and captured the garrison. The Allies were advancing from their bridgehead in Calabria, but only slowly, against stiff German resistance. Large German convoys had been seen moving south; they obviously had no intention of leaving the country without a fight. Knowing the Boche we should have expected this from the start. However, in spite of all this rather grim information our morale remained as high as ever, and we had not a doubt that our troops would advance, if not quite as fast as we had thought at first, nevertheless at great speed, and that they would be in the area within a month.

That evening reports reached the SBO that a large number of German troops had arrived and that an intensive effort to find us was to be expected at any time. He immediately issued a 'sauve qui peut' order and recommended us to make our way as best we could, either across the frontier into Switzerland or to join our own forces in the south.

Thanks to the assistance of the local inhabitants, every man who wanted it was kitted up in civilian clothing of sorts—an amazing example of generosity considering the shortage in Italy at that time. The behaviour of the villagers was magnificent from beginning to end, and countless invitations were extended to anyone who decided to wait there for the arrival of our own troops. Haylofts were made habitable, and cellars turned into living quarters, for those who remained in hiding in the area.

Michael and I had only one intention at this time, and that was to put as many miles as possible between

ourselves and a highly dangerous neighbourhood—and
the sooner the better. Toby Graham had attached himself to us and we three planned to keep together. After
a short discussion we agreed on the line we should take.
We considered that to cross into Switzerland, although
it was so close, would be a mistake, since we were
bound to be interned until there was a common frontier
between the Allies and the Swiss. We preferred the
alternative, which was to move towards our own troops
advancing north. We would go on walking down the
country to meet them as long as we could; but if we
were prevented, we would find a safe area and go into
hiding and wait for the advance to roll over us. Our
immediate objective, therefore, was to get away from
the relatively thickly populated and dangerous Po
valley, and make for the wild, mountainous country behind Genoa on the west coast.

This north-western tip of the Apennine range, which
runs like a hog's back for six hundred miles from north-
west of Genoa, down through the leg and into the boot
of Italy, lay about forty miles distant due south from
Parma. Once we had decided where we were going, we
wasted little time. We changed into civilian clothing
provided by the villagers, stuffed our pockets with what
tinned food we could carry, made our farewells to
Donald Shaw and Ian Fraser and set out.

2

We moved slowly and with caution, making wide détours round the villages. We were happy that at last the period of waiting was over and, with a sense of purpose in our minds, we faced the future with confidence. We had no doubt that we would succeed.

Michael was badly handicapped by the carbuncle under his arm and found the going heavy in the broiling heat. We used what little cover there was and avoided all tracks and roads. In this way we successfully skirted Fontanellato and approached the main Parma–Piacenza road. Since it was now past seven o'clock in the evening and we were all tired and hungry, we decided to put off tackling this major obstacle until the following morning, and started looking for a suitable farm where we could obtain food and shelter for the night. Our choice was typical of all farmhouses in this fertile area. The large pink-washed building was divided into living quarters in one half, and barns and cowe byres in the other, and the whole place had an appearance of solid prosperity, in contrast to the broken and squalid apathy of those we had seen around Naples. Chickens scratched in the yard, and fat cattle gazed solemnly at us as we approached the house.

We were received with great hospitality by the farmer and his wife, and although not desperately enthusiastic about having us in his house, he was quite willing to put us up for just the one night and provide us with a meal. He made it clear that he hoped we would leave first thing in the morning.

'I am a poor man, Signore. I already have my share of troubles and do not want more.'

We set his mind at rest, and in due course sat down to an excellent minestrone, with liberal supplies of home-made bread and butter. The inevitable vino was produced.

'It is poor wine, Signore,' said the farmer's wife apologetically, 'it has been a bad year.' But it tasted good to me, and when we left the family and retired to our beds in the hayloft above the cows, we glowed with an inner sense of well-being and alcoholic optimism. We slept in great comfort and left the farm soon after six the following morning.

We made a comic trio. The clothing, such as it was, was in all three cases much too small.

'I must say you cut a very dapper figure in your nattty suiting, Tony,' said Michael. My black striped trousers reached half-way between my knees and ankles, revealing a length of sock and army boots. My coat I carried slung over one shoulder. My grey silk shirt glistened in the sun. But my crowning glory was undoubtedly the hat. A large white panama with a black band, I wore it at a somewhat rakish angle tilted slightly forward.

'You look like a Hackney tailor on a Sunday, off to seduce his girl in Victoria Park,' said Toby.

'Well,' I retorted, 'you two look just as bloody silly.' Toby's coat left his wrists sticking out like broom handles, and his ridiculous conical felt hat was perched on his head like a schoolboy's cap. Michael insisted on tying string round his trousers just below the knee—navvy fashion—and in carrying his possessions in a large coloured handkerchief dangling from the end of a stick.

'With a week's growth of beard,' said Michael, 'we shall pass for Iteye peasants.' But he didn't convince anyone, least of all himself. There was no doubt about it, we looked exactly what we were—three British officers in disguise.

We approached the main road with caution. A hundred yards short of it, we stopped under cover of a clump of trees, so that we could observe the traffic and decide how best to get across. To our dismay, the southward flow of military vehicles had hardly a break in it. Occasionally the stretch of road would be empty for a minute or two, but just as we were on the point of moving down to cross it, there would be the sudden hum of engines, and another batch of lorries or motorcycles would appear round the corner. We couldn't decide what to do.

'I think we should just stroll casually across,' Michael said. 'After all, we are in civvies and these chaps won't take any notice of three peasants.'

'Don't be damned silly,' Toby retorted. 'We don't want to ruin our chances by reckless moves on the very first day.'

'We shall be here for ever if we don't do something.'

But caution prevailed, and it was the best part of an hour before there was a lull sustained enough to allow us to cross. We had just reached the other side when a solitary truck loaded with some half-dozen Germans, laughing and chatting in the back, swept past; but it didn't stop, so perhaps Michael was right and we needn't have worried so much.

Once over this first dangerous obstacle, our confidence increased, and, reaching a small side road, we swung happily along it, raising clouds of white dust at each footfall.

The sun was intensely hot and we were all sweating hard. We stopped at numerous farms for drinks of water, drawn from the well and deliciously cool. At this early stage of our venture, we preferred water to the vino which was inevitably produced when we asked for a drink. The peasants themselves scarcely drank water at all. When at work in the fields the farm labourer quenched his thirst by taking a swig at the vino bottle. This natural hydrophobia may well have been the result of the quality of the water available in most districts; it is certainly true, I believe, that the incidence of dysentery and other water-borne infections is remarkably low in Italy; though this may be compensated for, as in France, by a high incidence of alcoholism. Anyway, our thirst could not be quenched by vino alone, and so we drank vast quantities of water, a large percentage of which we lost in sweat a few minutes later.

The peasants themselves were delightfully curious when they met us. They were happy, childish people, whose only interest was in their own small plot of land, and whose knowledge of the world was restricted to a ten-mile radius round their home. Politics couldn't have interested them less, and the war was a remote unpleasantness which scarcely touched them at all. They were an emotional, cheerful people and their generosity was prodigal.

As the road wound its way out of the flat plain and into the foothills of the Apennines, houses became fewer, and the land more arid and rocky.

We were given an excellent meal at midday by a miller and his wife in their picturesque stone mill beside a small swift-running stream. The family possessed a wireless and we were delighted to find that the BBC service from London was well received. For the first time for a year we listened to the calm, unemotional voice of the announcer reading the news bulletin. There was little in it that concerned us, apart from a report that the Germans had attacked the Italian fleet on its way from Genoa and La Spezia to surrender to the Allied navies at Malta. This indicated that the Germans, as we had expected, were feeling savage about Italy's capitulation, and probably meant that our prospects of getting hospitality, food and shelter from the Italians would improve. They would insist that Italy was now an Allied nation, and the British would therefore be looked on as heroes, and, we hoped, treated as such. But the rest of the bulletin was much less satisfactory. There was no mention of the rumoured landings, nor of any phenomenal advances from the bridgehead. In fact the Allies had advanced just three miles in Calabria in the past three days, and the distance separating us from our own troops was still in the region of seven hundred miles.

During the afternoon we penetrated deeper into the hills. The going became harder, the gradient steeper and the sun hotter than ever. Poor Michael was noticing his lack of training and by four o'clock was lagging some fifty yards behind Toby and me. By this time we had covered about twenty miles and had reached a relatively wild area of rocky, barren hills with just an occasional farm here and there. It seemed safe enough; no German was likely to wander into such a remote and inhospitable countryside.

We accordingly set about finding a suitable place to lie up for a few days in anticipation of the landing in the north of Italy which we were still positive would be made. Our choice was a small impoverished-looking farm perched on the top of a hill and commanding a good view both of the only approach to it and of the surrounding slopes. The road on which we were walking had deteriorated into little more than a dusty track and seemed about to peter out altogether. It actually led to another small '*casa*' about a mile further on, and there it ended. This, and a similar stone building some two miles away to the north, were the only signs of life visible from the top of the hill.

Close to exhaustion, we slowly climbed the steep sides of the rock-strewn hill, picking our way through parched brown vines scattered among the stones. Michael was struggling up in his own time and Toby and I, on reaching the house, looked around for its owner.

'This is a grim-looking place,' said Toby, 'I'm not sure that it isn't empty.'

'Perhaps they got windy when they saw us coming.'

By this time we had moved round to the back of the farm where two large white yoke-oxen stood in the byre, chewing slowly and regarding us with a total lack of interest. Apart from these two beasts there was no sign of movement or habitation. There was no answer to our shouts and our voices echoed through the buildings.

'Well, where the devil do we go from here?' I said, and as I spoke I noticed a slight movement in the shadow of the lean-to barn. On closer inspection we could see two figures—a small wizened man and his wife. They stood anxiously together, fearfully watching and waiting to see what we wanted.

' '*Giorno, Signore.*'

'*Siamo Inglesi,*' we replied. 'We should like, if it is possible, to stay here for a few days. There is no need to have fear; we are good men.'

The two old people came out from the shadows, hesitated for a moment, and then the wife said:

'You are welcome, Signore. But I expect you are hungry. I will prepare some minestra; and you, Angelo,' she said, turning to her husband, 'bring some wine for the English signori.'

'*Si, si, Maria, subito.*'

Within minutes we were all the best of friends. The vino flowed and our Italian improved with every glass.

After the meal the old farmer showed us our sleeping quarters.

'We have no extra beds in the house,' he said, 'but out here in the *fienile* you will be warm. The hay is soft and my wife will give you some covers. I am very pleased to have you here, Inglese, and you may stay as long as you like. And now would you like to hear the radio?'

Yes, indeed we would. This was a stroke of luck, finding a radio in such an isolated spot!

'Well, but no, Signore, the wireless is not here in my house, but a relative of mine has one in a village not far from here. We could walk it quickly; it is really no distance.' Toby and I said we would like to go, but Michael, who was quite knocked up by the day's journey, wisely decided to stay behind and rest.

The old farmer had a short but lively argument with Maria and then the three of us set off along the hillside. The old man rattled on about farming problems, the price of tobacco and the shortage of every necessary commodity. He walked barefoot.

'My last pair of boots wore out in 1940,' he told us. 'No one round here has had a pair of boots or shoes since before this bloody war. Mussolini was stupid. He did much for Italy until he clamoured for an empire.

Abyssinia was the turning point. Life has got progressively worse for poor men, such as me, ever since. *Bastarde!*' he added, and spat expressively.

We walked steadily over the hills for more than an hour, and eventually, in the fast-gathering dusk, dropped down into a valley and arrived at a small group of stone houses and a church. The farmer led us to a house with a light in the window and a sign above the door saying 'Licensed for the sale of Wines, Tobacco and Salt'. With a flourish and a shout he ushered us into the bar of what was obviously the village pub.

Some seven or eight peasants were sitting round a table playing cards. The smoke from their pipes curled lazily through the beams of the oil lamp, and half-empty mugs of wine were scattered indiscriminately among the cards. The scene might, for all the world, have been set in some remote English village, except that the inhabitants took rather more notice of the strangers than English yokels would have done, and not one of them had seen a razor for at least a week. But they were a cheerful company and welcomed us royally. Our health was pledged in the local vino, a raw red vintage, with little to recommend it beyond its alcoholic properties. No Germans had been seen anywhere in the area, they said, and everything was going on nicely. Undoubtedly the Allies would arrive shortly—one week, maybe two, but certainly not much longer.

'Evidently nothing can stop the famous *"Ottava Armata" del Generale Montgomery,* the best army in the world.' We found this almost personal interest in Montgomery and the 8th Army, which was displayed by Italians of all classes, most intriguing. Since this particular army had virtually been solely responsible for Italy's defeat, their solicitude seemed even more remarkable. One of the most powerful propaganda write-ups I have ever read was an article about the 8th Army published on the day Tunis fell and still some four months before Italy's capitulation. It was printed in the Rome daily newspaper *Il Popolo*, and it explained at great length that only an army such as this with its magnificent fighting qualities, its high morale and incredibly efficient leadership could ever have defeated the gallant and noble 'Wolves of Tuscany'!

After we had been chatting away for some time we, and the entire company, were taken into a small parlour at the back of the building. Here Toby and I settled ourselves by the wireless and, after much juggling with the various switches and knobs, managed eventually to tune in to an Allied programme broadcast, I believe, from Algiers. The batteries needed charging and the reception was poor, but after ten minutes or so of Crosby records and Glen Miller music the American announcer read the news. We were on the edges of our chairs at once: after a preliminary bombardment from the sea and from the air, the newscaster informed us, a huge Allied armada had approached the Italian coast and a successful landing had been accomplished at . . . but at this climactic point the reception faded, and Toby and I were left literally hopping with frustration and anxiety to know where the Allies had landed.

'This may be what we have been waiting for,' I said to Toby, my voice quivering with excitement. 'It's sure to be in the Genoa area. It's the only sensible place.'

'I shouldn't be too optimistic,' said Toby, 'it may be miles away.'

After a spell of frantic retuning the announcer's voice gradually returned, '. . . and although the fighting on the beach-head is very severe our forces are advancing and the fall of Salerno is imminent.'

'Where is Salerno?' asked Toby.

'South of Naples,' I said, 'bloody miles away at the other end of the country.'

'I don't like the sound of that "heavy fighting". The Boche has obviously decided to stay and fight. It may be weeks before we break out of the beach-head.'

'You never know. Once the first battle is over, we may sweep everything before us.'

But however hard we tried to cheer ourselves up, it was two crestfallen men who walked back with the old farmer in the moonlight, and the track seemed never-ending. Michael was sitting in the kitchen with Maria.

We told him the news. Taking a pocket diary from his coat he turned to a small map of Italy. After a moment's calculation he announced with mock formality.

'Gentlemen, Salerno is approximately eight hundred miles from here as the crow flies.'

We stayed with those two delightful, hard-working people for a week, hoping each day to hear the news of a further landing somewhere in the north; but gradually we had to accept the fact that the possibility of any such landing was remote. It was Michael who finally forced us to look at our situation squarely.

'I think the time has come,' he said one morning, 'to decide what we're going to do. The alternatives remain the same, but it's no longer simply a question of walking for a week or two until we reach our troops. They're still a hell of a long way away, and their advance will probably be slow. On the other hand, to reach Switzerland, we shall have to cross the northern plains and the frontier, both of which are by now undoubtedly teeming with Boche.'

We discussed the problem from all angles, and eventually came to an unanimous decision. We would head south, start walking, cover as much of the distance as we could, and then find some likely spot about twenty miles ahead of the armies, and lie up there and let the Allied advance engulf us. It sounded simple and straightforward enough.

When we told the old man that we should be leaving on the following morning he seemed genuinely sorry to lose us.

'It would be so much safer for you to stay here and wait until your armies arrive. My wife and I are poor people, Signore, but you are indeed welcome to what little hospitality we can offer.'

We thanked them both sincerely for their kindness to us and wrote a chit for them to give to the Allied Military Commander of the area after their liberation. 'This man and his wife rendered excellent assistance to three British officers—escaped POWs. Any recompense you can offer them will be most richly deserved.' We all signed it, giving our names, ranks and the date. We told them to keep it well hidden until the Allies arrived, since if it were found by the Germans, swift and ruthless retribution would most certainly overtake them. They assured us that the wretched Tedeschi would never find it—or them. 'If they appear anywhere in these parts we shall go south into the mountains and return when they've gone.'

That evening Maria decided we should have a celebration to mark our impending departure. The old man walked off to the village and returned three hours later with some Chianti and a liberal supply of the local brew, and Maria prepared an enormous *polenta*. This was a dish peculiar to the peasants in the really poor mountain districts of Italy, and its main value lay in its bulk. It was really like a thick porridge, made from ground maize and water. The maize flour and water are put in a large cooking pot and simmered over an open wood fire for a considerable time. In a separate pan, meat or cheese, hashed up with liberal quantities of onions and tomato puree, is fried in olive oil. This is a sauce to add a little flavour to the *polenta,* which by itself, tastes of nothing at all.

At the appointed time we all seated ourselves round the rough kitchen table, which had been scrubbed until the wood shone white. We were each provided with a clasp knife, but no fork. Maria unhooked the steaming pot from above the fire and, holding it well out in front of her, upended it and turned the *polenta* out on to the table. A thick, smooth, yellow mass spread slowly towards us, covering an area of about four square feet. Within minutes it had set firm. At the centre of this expanse the meat sauce was piled into a small heap. We sat and stared at this incredible concoction, waiting for the next move.

With a sweep of her arm Maria invited us to start. *'Ecco amici, mangiate.'* Following her example we carved ourselves a large wedge of the *polenta*, spread a little of the sauce over its surface, and started to eat.

It was unlike anything I have ever had, before or since. Being of the consistency of thick blancmange, it was very easy to swallow, and in an odd way, it wasn't bad. Since we were all healthily hungry we soon cleared our respective square feet of table. When we had finished we felt quite replete, indeed somewhat distended.

For the rest of the evening we sat outside in the warm summer air, watching the sun go down and the moon rise, a great yellow globe from behind the mountains. I can remember perfectly the complete stillness and silence, and the feeling of well-being and contentment that pervaded our oddly mixed company. Over our vino I had a long conversation with Maria and it was then that I began to realize what a unique experience this trek of ours was going to be.

We were living on close terms with people whom, in the ordinary course of events, we should never have met, and whose character, philosophy and mode of living would have remained utterly outside our ken. It was an opportunity that comes the way of very few, and it was education in its fullest and richest sense. I consider myself lucky to have had the chance of getting to know such people; and, starting out as I did with an intense hatred of all things Italian, I very soon learned that the hard-working Italian peasant is a really delightful person. The ones we met on this walk of ours were the salt of the earth.

'Life has always been hard for us, Signore,' Maria said. 'Even before the war, there was always a shortage of most of the essential things of life. Coffee, sugar, clothes, and especially boots, were always scarce, and since 1940 there has been none at all for us. *Poveri noi*, the good things pass us by. But,' she added with a smile, 'we are content with our lot. Life is too short to be miserable. We have the land and it feeds us, and the wine is good. Children, Signore, keep you happy. I have had so many that I sometimes forget exactly how many. I was married young and was the mother of five by the age of twenty-one. Between times I worked in the fields. They are all grown up and gone away now. My sons are in the army and my daughters are married and living elsewhere. But they will be back soon to help Angelo and me in our old age. You need young limbs to work this hard, rocky soil.'

She asked me if I were married. I replied that none of us was.

'It is just as well, *giovani*. This must be a terrible time for your families and it is better that you have not left a young wife to weep over you. And in any case, you are too young.'

By ten-thirty the old man was in a magnificent state of alcoholic bravado.

'Madonna mia, just let me catch sight of one of those detestable Tedeschi and see what I shall do. I tell you, Inglese, no German shall set foot on my soil.' He was still in this truculent state when, at last, we bade them both goodnight and returned to our beds in the *fienile*.

For some time, as I lay in the hay waiting for sleep to come, I could hear Angelo's querulous voice echoing down the slope and across the valley as he sang exerpts from some of the better-known operas.

We awoke at five o'clock next morning to find Maria already busy about the farm. Old Angelo was still lying asleep on a heap of drying sweet-corn leaves in the yard.

'He has been there all night,' explained Maria. 'The vino is too much for him at times and he will wake feeling very sorry for himself. But come, I have *la colazione* for you.'

Breakfast was a meal few Italians ate, the peasants

largely because the necessary ingredients were lacking.
Bread and a cup of coffee was all they normally had
before starting their day's work. However, on this
occasion, three bowls of bread and milk were waiting
for us on the kitchen table.

As we were leaving, Maria pressed some loaves of
home-made bread and a large cheese into our pockets.

'You will need all the food you can get,' she said,
'and this will help you on your way.' When we eventually set off up the hillside, the two old people stood at
the door.

'*Arrivederci Inglese, auguri.*'

'Goodbye,' we called back. 'We shall return one day
and repay you for what you have done. *Mille grazie.*'

'*Niente, niente.*'

When we had gone some three hundred yards we
turned to look back at the house; there they still were,
waving to us, an elderly couple, living on the borderline
of utter poverty, yet they had given us freely of their
hospitality, their kindness and their friendship—all at
considerable risk to everything they possessed, including
their lives.

3

We headed due south towards the Apennines,
making for the small town of Bardi, which, the old
man had told us, was some twenty kilometres away.

'Just ask from time to time,' he said, 'anyone will

tell you.' Having no map, we could do nothing else. He was quite right. By asking at various farms which we passed, we were shown the most direct route across the mountains; but estimates of the distance varied considerably, and were rarely given in kilometres.

'It is so many hours' walking,' they would say, or 'You will reach it shortly if you follow this track.' We very soon found that these calculations were totally unreliable; and on many occasions, journeys which should, in local opinion, have taken two hours, kept us going at full stretch all day. But however fickle and faulty was their assistance in these matters, the peasants proved most useful in many others, not least being the excellent local intelligence screen they provided. To a man, they were terrified of the Germans, and small wonder; stories of rape and pillage in other areas had put the fear of God into these timid and childlike people. Consequently if, on approaching a village, we could see the men peacefully working in the fields or the women and children in the streets, it was a positive guarantee that no German was within miles of the place.

We made a point of speaking to everyone we met, or rather everyone we met made a point of speaking to us, and the conversation invariably went something like this.

' *'Giorno—da dove venite?'* (Hallo, where do you come from?)

'*Siamo Inglesi. Veniamo da vicino Piacenza.*' ('We are English and we come from the Piacenza area.)

'*Dove andate?*' (Where are you going?)

'To the south.'

'*Perchè?*'

'Because we are going to meet the Allied troops.'

Then we would ask:

'*Che sono alcuni Tedeschi in queste vicinanze?*'

'*No, niente Tedeschi.*'

At this point they would launch into a violent diatribe about the wickedness and cruelty of all Fascists and Germans.

'*Eh, ma. Buon giorno, auguri.*' And back to their work they would go.

For the first few days we found the journey hard. We weren't yet fully acclimatized to such tough hill walking, and by each evening we were ready to drop. Farms were not difficult to find, and although the extent of their hospitality varied considerably, we managed to obtain a hot meal each evening and a bed under cover. In addition, on most days we got some sort of bread and cheese for lunch.

We decided that, since this walk might well develop into a pretty lengthy and, in due course, possibly dangerous business, we stood a far greater chance of success if we were as fit as possible. The two obvious essentials, if we were to achieve this, were plenty of food and sleep.

Michael's view was that 'any bloody fool can eat and sleep rough', and Toby and I most heartily agreed with him. At the end of each day's walking, therefore, and while there were still a few hours of daylight, we started looking for a suitable farmhouse for the night, and we were invariably lucky. Usually we avoided the prosperous-looking places and made, instead, for some peasant's smallholding or little farm. They, we felt, were unlikely to betray us, whereas in the larger houses there was always the chance of meeting some ex-Fascist who would be only too happy to turn us over to the nearest German unit as we lay asleep in his barn. So we foreswore the chance of eating better and lying more comfortably for the good, solid reliable *polenta,* minestrone and pastaschuita, and a warm, if not always salubrious, bed in the hayloft or 'with the beasts'.

How well I remember the glorious feeling of freedom on that first week's walking. It was not merely freedom from capitivity that brought such elation, but the freedom from all the cares and worries of the world. We carried all our possessions in our pockets. We were beholden to no man and were responsible only to ourselves. Our future lay in our own hands and depended on our common sense, ingenuity and physical strength.

We faced a challenge which any fit young man with a taste for adventure would willingly have accepted. The going was rough; but, picking our way along rocky mountain tracks, fording ice-cold streams, sometimes up to our waists, beneath a cloudless blue sky, our faces and arms were soon burnt to a deep mahogany and our bodies quickly became lean and hard. Our natural enjoyment at exploring little-known parts of a foreign country, without a penny in our pockets, and depending for food and shelter on our own resourcefulness, was sharpened by the added spice of danger which was never far away. If we weren't actually being hunted, nevertheless a stray German patrol could surprise us at any time of day or night, and we had to be ready to meet it.

Facing trouble during the day did not worry us unduly; but the possibility of being rounded up while we were asleep at night was a constant anxiety. We always thoroughly investigated the hay-barns and cow-sheds which were our usual sleeping quarters; making sure there was a second exit, either a window or another doorway; and we sited our beds in the hay so that we could not be seen immediately by anyone entering, and also so that we had a clear run to the other exit if we had to make a dash for it. As an added precaution Michael steadfastly refused to take his boots off at night. For some time Toby and I tried to persuade him that this was not really necessary, and that his feet would suffer for it; but our protests ceased from the moment when Michael did, for once, take a boot off to remove a stone. We were in a small confined barn at the time!

Michael wore glasses. Indeed without them he could hardly see at all, but he refused to sleep in them; before settling down he would go through the ritual of removing them and placing them at some point on the hay within arm's reach. The risks this involved were vividly illustrated one night. We had been disturbed in the early hours by the excited barking of the farm dog. We were all ready to make a hasty exit in case of trouble, when Michael whispered hoarsely, 'I can't find my glasses!' and started a feverish search among the hay.

I stationed myself by one door and Toby by the other and we anxiously kept watch. The dog was still barking furiously, and I thought I could hear footsteps and voices coming from beyond the farm. All this time Michael was thrashing about in the hay, systematically pawing every inch. He found them eventually, but by then the furore had died down. From that night on, he tied them to his wrist with a length of string.

We soon developed the habit of being able to sleep deeply and dreamlessly throughout the night, but of waking instantly and completely at the first sign of danger. By nature I don't think any of us was likely to find danger where there was none, and unnecessary anxiety on this score did not therefore affect our tranquil state of mind.

Our day started early. Living quite frequently in the same barn *'colle bestie'*, as the Italians described it, it was inevitable that our hours should coincide with those kept by the animals, so that although we did not retire at dusk, we were always awake and up shortly after dawn. By 6 a.m. we were usually well on our way again. We rested for ten minutes or so every two hours, and spent about an hour at midday having lunch at some farm. Around four-thirty in the afternoon we started looking for somewhere to spend the night. In this way we put in a good nine to ten hours' walking every day, while the distance we covered increased as our state of fitness improved.

But it was difficult country, and by the end of the day we were exhausted. Our legs felt like lead, and conversation was out of the question; we needed every scrap of energy for the sheer physical effort of putting one foot in front of the other. Michael, who must have felt far worse than Toby and I, carried on magnificently. The carbuncle under his arm seemed to be no smaller, and it must have sapped a good deal of his strength. The whole mass was suppurating horribly, and in a somewhat inadequate way we tried to keep it dressed. We boiled a strip of Toby's shirt at a farm, and this, together with a piece of cloth impregnated with the excellent Germolene from my tin, we applied to Michael's side and strapped into position. We didn't forget the therapeutic value of ultra-violet rays, and so for two hours each day, when the sun was at its height, we bound his arm up behind his head, and in this awkward position Michael walked, bare-chested, the sun and air doing their work as he moved along. Either because, or in spite of, this treatment, there was some improvement in his condition, and after a week or so the lump began to subside. The carbuncle never cleared completely during the whole trek, but by the end of the second week Michael was no longer incapacitated by its presence, and he was soon as fit as Toby and I.

Feet were quite a problem for two members of the party. Michael's sweated a lot, and, until they hardened up, he suffered a series of blistered heels and soles which very nearly crippled him. Toby was even less fortunate; while at Fontenellato he had cut down the uppers of his army boots. As part of his disguise for his previous escape, they were all right, but for hard walking over rough country they were terrible. His feet blistered so badly that on more than one occasion his socks were soaked in blood. However, his feet gradually became accustomed to this form of refined torture, and within a few weeks they had healed and hardened up perfectly. I was luckier. My boots, though not new, had been mended and hobnailed three days before we had left camp; in any case, my feet don't sweat; and during the whole of the walk, although they were often sore, they never blistered once. An army may well march on its stomach, but its feet must take some part in the proceedings, and when contemplating excursions such as this, one cannot underestimate the importance of being well shod.

During the first week we moved with excessive caution. We avoided even the most minor roads, and made our way entirely by mule track or directly across country. As the days passed, our eyes and instincts sharpened, so that before long we could pick out the slightest movement in the landscape at a very great distance. We walked so that the sound of our footsteps was deadened by the grass and our movements hidden in what shadows were cast across the countryside. These precautions, though they may sound over-elaborate, were not a sign of 'windiness'; it was simply that we were taking no chances.

Our first night out from the farm at Mariano we stayed at a small *paesino* or community, called Contile. It consisted of a jumble of about twelve stone and slate buildings and a beautiful little church, perched at about 3,500 feet on the top of a very steep hill. There was no road into it, just an interminable spiral track, and as we wound our way up we passed a train of mules winding their way down.

When we finally reached the village we were wel-comed by a charming but incredibly dirty old lady. Her cottage, though of only two rooms, was as full of photographs as most Italian households and we were shown these at once. She seemed to have had a truly enormous family, all of whom had departed. Two sons, she explained, had been in America since 1925, and one daughter had married a man from a neighbouring *paese* and emigrated to Australia just before the war.

She prepared an excellent minestrone and, accom-panied by what must have been a large proportion of the fly population of the district, we sat down at the kitchen table to eat. They swarmed everywhere and it was difficult to avoid swallowing some with every mouthful. If a student of hygiene had been with us, he would have had a nervous breakdown. Yet in spite of the filth and the complete absence of sanitation, both more or less universal, there seemed to be very little illness among the peasant population and the children appeared completely immune to the hordes of insects which accompanied them everywhere they went.

After our meal we wandered through the village and came to the church. From the outside it looked as roughly constructed as the other buildings; but inside it was exquisitely decorated. The effigy of the Madonna and Child was almost lifelike in the perfection of its delicate colour and moulding. While we were gazing at it with admiration the village priest approached us. He was tall and dignified and he spoke with a peculiarly soft and tranquil voice which we found to be common among the priests we met on the trip.

'*Buona sera, amici.* Would you care to look round? You are Catholics? No? Well, no matter, you are welcome just the same.' He conducted us round with great solicitude, pointing out a fine carving here and a beautiful painting there. At the end of the tour he invited us into his house, which adjoined the chapel, to drink some wine with him.

This was our first meeting with a priest on our walk and was the beginning of a very useful liaison with these excellent people which continued throughout the adventure. We were immediately struck by the cleanliness and comfort of his house compared with the surrounding squalor. He explained a little of his job to us as we sat in his living-room.

'You see, Signore, I am not merely the spiritual father of my flock here in Contile; I am also their adviser and father on pretty well everything else. They bring all their problems to me. When they are sick or hurt, I tend them, as there's no doctor within a day's journey of this place. Family quarrels are brought to me for arbitration, and disobedient sons and daughters are sent to me for punishment and guidance. I am called Father, and I am their father, and they are all my children. They're fractious and disappointing at times as all children are, but they have big hearts, Signore, and they are very lovable people. I would not want to spend my life in any other place.'

He gave us a half-inch map of Emilia and Tuscany. It was an Italian motor touring map, and as well as all classes of road, it showed remarkably accurate contours; as soon as we left Contile the following morning we realized what a tremendous help it was going to be to us. We no longer progressed in a zigzag fashion, or in a series of great arcs, but moved more or less in a straight line towards our immediate destination for the day.

During the whole of this period, while we were still in the foothills of the Apennines, our route took us diagonally across the river valleys and roads which ran up from the Lombardy plain to the main ridge, on the other side of which lay the coast towns, Genoa, La Spezia and Livorno. Owing to this particular conformation of the country, we advanced, as it were, over a vast sheet of corrugated iron, climbing up the steep hillside from a valley only to find at the summit that a further valley lay on the other side, and beyond that another hill, and so on as far as the eye could see and beyond—a most disheartening prospect. At lunch-time we were foolish enough to measure our progress on the map. After six hours of continuous slogging, during which we must have walked at least fifteen miles, we found we had actually advanced three miles. This seemed a miserable return for the expenditure of so much energy, and did nothing for our impatience to get on.

However, although the route was hard and slow,

I'm sure we were wise to stay well up in the mountains. If we had gone twenty miles farther east into lower, flatter country, no doubt we could have moved faster, but the risk of encountering the Boche would have been that much greater. So we stayed in the mountains, cursing and sweating, and making slow but steady progress. At least we were perfectly safe. Indeed, we could have given a whole army the slip in those barren hills; and the only time exceptional caution was called for was when we crossed the main roads that run through to the coast.

We approached the first of these towards the end of the day's walking from Contile. Standing on the crest of one of the interminable ridges, we looked down and saw the white ribbon of road about four hundred feet below us. Beyond it, the slope continued down a steep drop to the valley of the Parma river, and beyond the river soared another hill. The slope on both sides of the road was quite bare, without a scrap of cover under which to approach or leave it. As we pondered the problem, we heard a low rumble of traffic and a large German convoy appeared and slowly ground its way up the road towards the Cisa Pass away on our right. We were tired and hungry and, as it was already past five o'clock, we decided to put off crossing until the morning. Then we should be refreshed and better fitted to tackle it. Accordingly we made our way to a small house, perched on the hillside about two hundred yards from the road in a clump of stunted pines. The only sign of habitation was the thin veil of smoke rising from its chimney stack and a few hens scratching in the dust outside the door.

We were met, without much enthusiasm, by a strong-looking woman of about forty and her son of eighteen.

Neither the woman nor the boy were of the usual peasant type, and the house lacked the customary patch of cultivated land around it. In fact, their presence in this isolated spot was at first a bit of a mystery; but they were an unattractive pair, and we were content to eat the meal they gave us without being talkative. From the first, we kept an eye on the son. I didn't much like the look of him, but whatever fears we may have had of a treacherous move on his part were quite unnecessary. He was a miserable specimen, physically and mentally, and I doubt whether he would have had the guts to creep out of the house and stop one of the German trucks on the road below, even if he had had the inclination. Under the baleful glare of the three large ruffians seated at his kitchen table, the poor lad wilted visibly, and eventually crept away to a dark corner. There he sat huddled over a book, though he could not possibly have been able to see to read it.

After the meal the mother, who had been completely silent the whole time, thawed out a little, and gradually an uneasy sort of conversation started. At first she was obviously undecided whether to believe our story, and I am sure that for some time she was convinced we were German; although what she thought three German soldiers were doing in tattered civilian clothing and wandering abroad like tramps I can't imagine. However, her suspicions gradually evaporated; and, slowly and hesitatingly, she began to answer our questions about herself and her son.

'I am a widow, Signore. My husband died some years ago and until recently I have lived with my son in Parma. Two years ago I entered him at the university to study medicine. Unfortunately he did not pass any of his exams and would soon have been forced to join the army. He is not a strong boy and the army would have killed him. After the Armistice it became imperative to leave Parma, as the Germans were taking all the young men away to Germany as forced labour. So we rented this small *casa*, and now Roberto can study his books in peace.'

His mother hereupon cast a look of great affection on the unfortunate youth still sitting in utter dejection in the corner. I tried to picture Roberto in a few years' time as a qualified doctor, and silently prayed that I would never be taken ill in Italy.

Her problem, and its solution, was typical of those faced by many Italian families. And as usual in this country it was the women who faced the eventualities, made the decisions and shouldered the burdens, while their menfolk fluttered ineffectually in the background wringing their hands and wallowing in self-pity. I have no doubt that much of Italy's post-war recovery is due to the practical common sense of its women.

During the whole of that evening and far into the night the traffic continued to roll in a seemingly endless stream towards the west coast. From what we learnt later our interpretation of this activity appeared to be correct: the Germans were hastily building fortifications in the mountains behind the large west coast ports against a possible Allied landing from the sea. We listened to the roar of the convoys as we lay in the hayloft that night; and each fresh group of vehicles that passed seemed to add miles to the distance we should have to walk to reach our own troops. After all these strenuous days, the gap between ourselves and the Allied armies seemed as great as ever. What was more, if the going did not improve soon, it looked as if we would still be miles away from our destination when the first winter snows fell and made the mountains impassable.

4

We left the house soon after first light and moved along the hillside until we could see a fair stretch of the road to the left and right. Not a sound could be heard in the still morning air and the road itself was deserted. Half running, half sliding, we cascaded down the slope and were across the road in a matter of seconds. After the night's worries and fears it was something of an anticlimax.

Another ten minutes of scrambling down the steep side of the valley beyond brought us to the river bed. During the summer months the river was a mere silver thread, ten feet wide and only a few inches deep; but with a week of the coming of the winter rains, we were told, it would be a very different matter. The harmless, shallow stream would become a raging torrent, two hundred feet wide and many feet deep, and crossing it, except by the bridges, would be virtually impossible. As it was, we simply paddled across, our feet crunching over the pebbles bleached by the sun. On the far side there was a crystal-clear pool, so blue and sparkling and inviting that we stripped off and had our first bath since leaving Fontanellato. It was early still, yet the sun was already hot and bright, and its rays glistened and danced on the stream and on the water drying on our backs. We lay sunning ourselves on the warm stones and let the beauty of the place envelop us. The grandeur of the mountains, the rippling of the water and, above all, the riot of colour from the deep blue of the sky to the golden peaks in the distance was indeed a spectacle to refreshen mind and body. It was with a feeling of inner elation and happiness that we set out again on our journey.

For the next five days our progress was steady, if not exactly spectacular, on average about sixteen kilometres a day as the crow flies. The country became no easier; in many ways in fact, it grew considerably harder. The hills were steeper and grass gave way to rocks. Houses were more difficult to find and the food in them deteriorated in quality and quantity. Worst of all, it started to rain. The first break in the weather occurred on the night of Saturday, 17 September. I remember it well. In the gathering gloom of the rain clouds we arrived at a small ragged village tucked away in a fold of the mountains. It was five o'clock in the afternoon and the cobbled street was empty; but in spite of the air of desertion the houses were occupied, for we could see faces peering furtively through the windows at us as we passed. Depression seemed to have settled firmly on what was probably a cheerful community in normal times. Presently we learnt why. Early that morning, a German patrol had descended on a neighbouring village, only two kilometres away, and had systematically searched every house and barn. In addition to all the livestock and anything else of value they could lay their hands on, they had rounded up all the men between the ages of fifteen and fifty and any of the girls with a claim to beauty and driven off with the lot.

'*Questi Tedeschi!* They have taken everything, even the yoke oxen,' we were told. 'Now we have nothing left, nothing at all, and no young people to work the land. It is terrible; we shall all starve.'

It was with no great enthusiasm, therefore, that we made this village our resting place for the night, and it was with no great enthusiasm that the village received the news that we were going to stay with them. They saw in us the omens of a terrible retribution by the Germans on the whole community if we were found there, which was probably quite true.

However, from our point of view the place was suitable. The villagers were far too frightened to venture far from their houses and their very nervousness acted as an excellent warning system. Any suspicious movement within miles would start a panic, which we should be certain to hear; besides, it looked like rain. So we decided to stay; and reluctantly, with much vehement protesting, we were provided with food and a bed in the usual hayloft. For our unwilling host we chose a young man who, although of some standing in the village, seemed even more demoralized than the rest. He regarded us with ill-disguised horror and visibly quailed when we told him we proposed to sleep in his barn.

'But, Signore, the Tedeschi will come, and may find you. Then what will happen to me, I will be shot; they will burn down my home. Please, Signore, go somewhere else, anywhere but here.'

We were in no mood to respect his honest terrors, and stood on his threshold as immovable as three rocks.

'We're not asking much from you, and if you don't open up that barn at once, we shall burn the bloody thing down ourselves and save the Germans the trouble. Now get going.'

Torn between present fear of us and future fear of the Tedeschi, he gave in and, literally wringing his hands, led the way to the large brick-built barn which was filled almost to the roof with hay. As we inspected the place the first heavy drops of rain pattered down. Within an hour the drumming on the roof drowned our conversation and the doors and shutters rattled furiously in the wind. The outlook for the morrow was grim indeed, but for the moment we were warm and dry. Sinking deeper into the hay we very soon fell into a dreamless sleep.

Some hours later, in obedience to that extra sense which the hunted develop, I woke up. It was still pitch dark and, although it had stopped raining, the wind was high and whistled dismally round the corners of the old barn. What had triggered off that alarm bell in my sleeping mind? I sat up in the hay and listened. A moment later the door creaked on its latch and I saw the flicker of a lantern. Someone started to climb the ladder leading to the top of the stack where we were lying.

By this time Michael and Toby were also awake and the three of us stood in the shadows among the rafters, our hearts pounding and our mouths dry. Slowly the light came towards us. First we saw an arm holding the flickering lantern aloft and then a head— not, as it happened, the head of some storm trooper, but the head of our host. In a stuttering whisper he said:

'When the moon rises you must go. The Tedeschi—
they are here!'

After a slight pause while we digested this shattering
news, the Italian, the hand which held the lantern
trembling in a most disconcerting manner so that at any
moment I expected him to drop it, again urged us to
go before it was too late.

'Please hurry. They will be here soon and will find
you, and then the most terrible misfortunes will befall
me for hiding you.'

'They *will be* here, did you say? You told us at first
that they *were* here. Which is it? Are they in the
village?'

'They're not actually in the village yet, Signore, but
a report has come that they were seen on the road
leading here just a short while back. It is certain that
they will be here very soon.'

'Who brought this story?'

'I do not know exactly, Signore. It is a rumour in the
village. But certainly they are *nelle vicinanze*.'

We knew from past experience that '*nelle vicinanze*'
covered an area of twenty square miles around and on
reflection we felt inclined to take the whole story with
a pinch of salt.

'We think it unlikely,' we told our shivering host,
'that the Germans will be here tonight, and we have
no intention of leaving before the morning. And now, if
you will close the door after you when you leave, we
can get some sleep.'

Almost beside himself with terror, he did as he was
told and we lay down again. But, just in case, we left
the barn at first light and were well away from the
village by 6 a.m.

It was Sunday, so we moved out of the immediate

area by crossing into the next valley. We had laboured full well on the previous six days, and on the seventh we most definitely intended to rest, come what might.

The morning had been grey and cold, but by the time we reached Aveta the sun was once more breaking through the clouds. Here we washed and shaved, the first shave for nearly a week, and were provided with an excellent meal. But there was nowhere in Aveta suitable to spend the night, so during the afternoon we walked on a short distance to the next village. I do not remember the name of the place or very much about it, except that it possessed a church and that this particular Sunday happened to be the fiesta of its patron saint.

We arrived at just the right moment. The processions and the more solemn ritual of the day were over and the villagers, dressed in their best clothes, were well into the noisier part of the celebrations. We were welcomed in a most cheerful and vociferous manner and immediately invited to join in the fun. None of us was the type to miss a party, and the unexpected one is always the best. Certainly that Sunday afternoon and evening turned out to be one of the rowdiest and most enjoyable binges I have ever had! There was singing and dancing in the streets to a two-man accordion band and a continuous supply of vino and sweet cakes of every description. The tempo was fast and furious, and relaxed only for a few minutes occasionally while the dancers revived their dry throats and tired limbs with the excellent local brew. Mike, Toby and I kept going with the best, revelling in the delightful contrast to our gruelling efforts of the previous weeks. It was ages since we had each had an arm round a pretty young girl, laughing and full of life and spirit, and very pleasant indeed we found it.

The celebrations ended at midnight, by which time the revelry had transferred itself to the largest house in the village. It was packed to overflowing, and the noise was deafening, but we were somehow persuaded to sing a song in English to the assembled company. We could think of nothing suitable at first; but eventually we gave a fair rendering of one of the less reputable barrack room ballads. The evening was nearing its end anyway, everyone was pretty high and no one understood English, which was probably just as well, but we sang with much gusto to the accompaniment of the accordion, and to the thunderous applause of all present. When the party eventually broke up, we were given an excellent sleeping place in a small shed, with dried leaves instead of the usual hay.

As a result of the night's debauchery we overslept, and it was later than usual when, to the good wishes and farewells of pretty well the entire village, we set out on the next stage of our journey.

The weather was bad and, what with the rain and our hangovers, we had a wretched day. The countryside, which, in the sunshine, had looked ravishingly beautiful, now assumed a cloak of gloom and barrenness. The mountain tops were hidden in cloud and the whole landscape presented a picture of utter desolation. In a very short time we were wet through, our boots squelched, water trickled down our backs and our state of misery was such that it was almost humorous.

During the next six days it rained incessantly. As usual, we found a welcome with a meal and a warm hay bed every evening. Our clothes dried on us, so that after twenty minutes or so spent lying in the *fienile*, a small cloud of steam could be seen rising from our bodies. By the following morning we were quite dry. For a few delicious minutes after waking I would revel in the warmth and comfort, made all the sweeter by the knowledge that within a short time I would be slogging away up some mountainside, soaked to the skin once more.

Although one looks back with horror at this perpetual state of dampness and chill, none of us caught so much as a cold and we never appeared to be any the worse for our wettings.

On 21 September we had covered over one hundred kilometres in a straight line from our starting point at Mariano. We had reached a position almost due south of Modena and were still walking metaphorically down the hog's back of the Apennines. Some of the highest peaks in the whole range lie in this area and on the morning of the 22nd we reached Monte Cimone. This mountain, more than six thousand feet high, towers over the rest of the range by one thousand feet or more, and dominates the landscape. We found that, whichever way we turned, the conformation of the country led us inevitably to the foot of this monster. There was no escaping it, and no way round it, unless we made a time-consuming twenty kilometre détour, and this we couldn't face.

At last there was a let-up in the weather, and this made us all the more impatient to press on. Drawn towards Cimone as by a magnet, we eventually found we had no alternative but to mount a frontal attack on the citadel—an attack that would take us right over the summit and possibly give us a tricky descent on the other side. From a distance the slopes appeared almost vertical, and it was difficult to see how we were going to make our way up them; but as we got nearer the foot, the crags and crevices turned out to be less dangerous than they had seemed. When we paused to get our breath, we found to our surprise that we had already climbed a considerable way, and the final assault on the summit lay ahead of us.

The whole north face of Cimone was in deep shadow, and we were very thankful to be out of the sun as we toiled on up. That last stretch took us three hours; then, at last, we found ourselves crossing the crest. But whatever the expenditure of energy, it was worth it. The panorama stretched from horizon to horizon and as far as eye could reach. Behind us lay Emilia with the Po valley just discernible in the mist. Before us lay Tuscany with the Apennine range twisting its way south and forming a high thick wall between the fertile valleys and plains running east to the Adriatic and west to the Mediterranean.

As we gazed down on this splendid scene, our eyes settled on the peaks and hills in the south—peaks and hills we should be climbing in a few days, on another stage of our journey. For us, the summit of Monte Cimone was a sort of watershed; on the far side lay the unknown, which we both longed for and feared.

In fact, the southern slopes of the mountain were very much easier. Rocks gave away to moorland grass curving downwards in a series of sweeps. The lower reaches were thickly wooded, first with pines and then, lower still, the characteristic Tuscan chestnut groves.

To our great surprise, we presently came to a large Swiss-style chalet. It was a most imposing building and from it a good motor road wound its way down into the valley. We gazed at it with some suspicion, and even as we watched, the sound of voices floated up to us. A man with a Dalmatian dog came out on to the verandah, followed by four or five other men. The sun glinted on the fire-arms which two or three of them wore slung over one shoulder. Each one wore a bandolier of cartridges. They were all dressed in civilian clothing and spoke Italian.

In spite of the peaceful atmosphere which pervaded the party, we had to nerve ourselves to stroll casually down the slope towards them. Our appearance caused a certain amount of consternation. Two of the men immediately disappeared into the house. Two others, holding their guns at the 'port', came down the steps and stood waiting for us. We stopped some twenty yards from them, and there was a long tense silence.

'*Cosa volete?*—what do you want here?' It was the apparent leader of the party who spoke, a tall dark good-looking man of about thirty.

'We want nothing here. We are merely walking through the district.'

'*Dove siete*—of what nationality are you?'

'We are English. We are escaped prisoners of war.'

'*Ecco, amici*. Welcome, then; come inside.'

The scowls changed to smiles, the guns were lowered, and we were ushered into the chalet with many gestures of hospitality and pleasure. Wine was produced; we were invited to lunch with them, and over an excellent meal all was explained.

These men were deserted officers of the Alpini Regiment, the corps d'élite of the Italian army. Unlike most Italians, their interest in the war was still very much alive, and they told us that they were in the process of forming a guerrilla band to harry the Germans in the area. It was from many such groups of determined young men that large 'Partigiani' units were eventually formed.

'Perhaps tomorrow we shall fight, but today we are here for *La caccia.*' This so-called hunting expedition explained their presence in the chalet, which was, they told us, a winter sports *rifugio.* Cimone possessed some of the finest ski-slopes outside the Alps and was, apparently, very popular with Italian enthusiasts. The *rifugio* was kept well stocked with food and could accommodate thirty or forty people. It provided an ideal head-quarters for these renegade Alpini, who, in the intervals between planning their offensive, were having a thoroughly good time, shooting what game they could find or just lying in the sun. They even had a small car in which to drive down to the valley in search of female company or to revisit their homes for a day or two.

Although German security measures were becoming more stringent every day, they had not yet become so harsh as to make such trips dangerous. So, for the time being, these Alpini were having a lot of fun and were naturally reluctant to begin the unpleasant business of actual warfare. But I have no doubt that they got down to it eventually.

Before we left, Mike, Toby and I had to pose for a series of photographs surrounded by these partisans in embryo. Addresses were exchanged, and they insisted on our accepting a gift of three thousand lire, which at the rate then prevailing was a lot of money.

'You never know when you may need it,' their leader said. 'Money can work most things in Italy, and it may help you out of trouble some time. And now, Inglese, *auguri e arrivederci.* Perhaps after the war we shall meet again—and what a party that would be! Goodbye.'

The day was memorable in other ways, too. During the afternoon we made good progress over much easier countryside, and by five o'clock had reached a small picturesque village which was distinguished from the other mountain communities we had encountered by its air of prosperity. Choosing a mill, set a little apart on the outskirts, we were welcomed with enthusiasm by the miller herself, a widow, and her three boisterous daughters.

These girls were delightful company. The family was obviously comfortably off and the daughters had had the advantages of a good education. Their conversation was stimulating, and to us, starved of civilized female society for a long time, the evening was a rare pleasure. In the middle of it, there was a peremptory knock on the door. The eldest daughter went to answer it and her voice carried clearly to the rest of us sitting in frozen and expectant silence.

'*Buona sera, Carabiniere.* What can I do for you?'

Quietly and with the utmost efficiency and calm we were immediately led down to the cellars and hidden behind a pile of wine casks.

'Stay here,' the girls said, 'while we deal with the Carabiniere.'

For nearly an hour we heard the policeman's voice in the room above. He was there on some sort of official business, but we could not guess whether it concerned us in any way. Eventually the door was closed after him and we were called up from our hiding-place.

'It was only an enquiry about grain returns. But that one never stops talking, and we couldn't get rid of him any sooner.'

Their anxiety was understandable. The transitional period through which the Italian State was then passing left the role of the Carabiniere in some doubt. Their loyalty was to their King and country, but they were also pledged to maintain law and order in a kingdom ripe for anarchy and were therefore liable to obey the orders of whatever civil or military power administered their particular area. So that, for a short time at least, they were working with the Allied powers in the south, and with the Germans and the Italian Republican Government in the north. Carabiniere were armed and unpredictable, and both we and our helpers went to great lengths to avoid them.

5

Although up to now our journeying had been uneventful enough, circumstances were deteriorating steadily as the days passed. The ugly word *'Fascisti'* was being mentioned with increasing frequency, and we could no longer rely on a friendly attitude from every Italian civilian.

Mussolini had been rescued from his mountain prison by German paratroops, and, under the military protection of Kesselring's forces, the Rupublican Fascist Government had been established in the north of Italy. Bands of young thugs had been enrolled in the 'Blackshirt Militia', and a growing army of these detestable hooligans were engaged in a reign of terror, arresting and executing thousands of citizens and spreading an ever-widening net for escaped prisoners of war such as ourselves. They were a real danger to us, although, hated as they were, it was very unlikely that anyone would betray us to them. They just represented another enemy to contend with and a complication we could well do without.

In fact, our first serious trouble came not from the Fascisti, but from a German patrol.

On 27 September, after saying goodbye to the widow and her daughters at the mill, we climbed once more into the hills which formed a semi-circle to the north of Florence and other large towns in Tuscany. We were heading towards Firenzuola, a smallish place on the western side of the main Apennine range. The weather had completely broken and we plodded miserably through a high wind and driving rain, up into the mist which shrouded the mountain tops. Here we were moving 'blind', in a roughly south-easterly direction, and it wasn't until we came down out of the mist some hours later that we realized we were approaching a village of considerable size. The mule track we were following improved and widened, and within a few minutes we found ourselves walking along a road—the first we had used since leaving the farm at Mariano. Roads, we had always felt, might lead us into trouble and this one did.

We swung briskly round a corner. A young German paratrooper stood there with his machine-pistol trained on us.

'*Kommen Sie dann, aber schnell und mit die Hände hoch.*'

There was nothing for it but to obey, and the small procession started down the hill towards the sounds of voices which reached us, muffled, from the thickly wooded valley. Gradually my feeling of stunned unreality gave way to one of desperation. If we were going to avoid complete disaster, we should have to act quickly, for every minute brought us nearer to the rest of the German patrol.

Our guard, although the hand holding the weapon appeared steady enough, was very white around the gills. He was scarcely more than a boy and obviously as frightened and startled as we were ourselves. We walked as slowly as we dared and then I began to limp.

'*Moment bitte*,' I said, and stopped. 'It is my leg. I am lame and can go no farther for a moment.'

The German seemed to understand; he hesitated, and dropped the muzzle of his gun for a second. In a flash the three of us were upon him, tearing, twisting, throttling. The Schmeisser pistol rolled out of his reach. He opened his mouth to shout, but before any sound emerged Michael hit him over the head with a heavy lump of wood. We went on hitting him until at last he lay quite still in a twisted pitiful heap, his head hanging at an odd angle on his broken neck.

We turned and ran back up the hill and it was nearly an hour before we stopped to rest our bursting lungs and pounding hearts. I have never felt more tired or sick.

This horrible encounter cost us much valuable time, as we made a wide détour round the entire area. We had ventured too far down from the isolation of the Apennine peaks and had touched the fringe of fertile land surrounding Florence, which was being systematically plundered by the Germans. The locality was too dangerous, and in avoiding it we were forced some forty miles off our direct route south and away from almost all signs of habitation.

There were no farms at the height we were travelling, and the only people we came across were the occasional *carbonari* or charcoal burners. This industry was spread diffusely over most of the mountains of Tuscany, and its workers lived a peculiarly isolated and monk-like existence in their remote wooden huts. They were on duty for a month at a time, tending the mounds of brushwood and seldom seeing another human face. These mounds were most cunningly constructed, with the wood so placed that there was no sudden conflagration as in a normal bonfire, but a slow deliberate smouldering which, in the course of several weeks, transformed the interior of the mound into a heap to topgrade charcoal. This was collected in sacks and periodically taken down the mountain by mule-train. The shortage of coal was so acute that in many Italian towns charcoal was the only cooking fuel available.

The charcoal burners were a happy and independent breed. With no companion to talk to, they were inclined to sing to themselves as they went about their work, so that is was no unusual occurrence to hear snatches of song emanating as it were from the bald mountainside. We were received with the utmost cordiality by these men and generously invited to share their meagre rations and the shelter of their huts. The food was plain indeed—a half-dozen boiled potatoes, for instance —but we accepted it in the spirit in which it was offered, and in any case there was no other source available.

We spent two nights in this way, and they were among the worst of our journey. The weather was foul, the nights damnably cold, and we never got enough to eat. The floors of the huts were covered with a thin film of charcoal, and for blankets we used sacks. Our appearance by the morning was indescribable. Charcoal dust was in our eyes, ears and nostrils, and our beards, by this time grown to about an inch of stubble, were black and filthy. There was no water to wash in, apart from the incessant rain, so we stayed dirty, and I doubt if three more disreputable characters were ever seen.

On the third day, 30 September, we got back on to our intended route in the neighbourhood of Firenzuola, a town which was to be the scene of much bitter fighting a year later. The weather had temporarily improved and from ten kilometres away we could look down on the pink and white buildings reflecting the sunlight in the clear air. It was a most beautiful sight. Firenzuola lay at the end of a long wide valley which cut a swathe through the mountains. Farm houses were grouped in clusters on either side of the river and around them lay a patchwork quilt of cultivated land. It was a pleasure to set eyes once more on signs of civilization, and we stood for some minutes enjoying the scene before going down to cross the road and the river.

A few miles short of the town we came to a village which seemed a suitable stopping place for the night. We sought out the village priest, who gave us food and wine but regretted he had nowhere we could sleep. We were still discussing this when another visitor arrived. After a few minutes' conversation, the newcomer approached us and, speaking in perfect English, invited us to spend the night at his house.

'It is some distance from here,' he said, 'but I should be delighted if you would come with me.'

And so the four of us set off up the hillside, where half an hour's stiff climbing brought us to a small but beautiful villa set in an exquisite garden. Inside, we were faced with such luxury as we had not seen since leaving England.

'The bathroom is at your service,' he said. 'The water is hot, and I'm sure you would appreciate a bath.'

The running taps were music in our ears, and I could have shouted with happiness as I lay relaxing in the steamy warmth. Dirt and tiredness disappeared, and by the time we went down to dinner we were hardly recognizable as the three ruffians who had entered the house an hour earlier.

Our host was obviously greatly pleased to have us with him. He was an excellent talker, a man of intellect and breeding, and a remarkable philosopher. Towards the end of the evening he took us into his library where over cognac and cigars he spoke to us of his life.

'You may wonder, gentlemen, why I am living in this solitude surrounded by my books and with just one old housekeeper to talk to.'

Personally I could think of no nicer way of spending the time, but I kept quiet.

'You see,' he said, ' I have been virtually banished to this place since 1941. I am a poet, a Jesuit and a religious man, and the Fascists found some of my publications offensive. My property in Rome was confiscated, and this villa is, in effect, my prison. I spend my time writing, and praying that this war may end. Do not misunderstand me, gentlemen. I love my country and want nothing better than to see Italy great again. But I fear that misery and destruction will be her lot for some time yet. It is a tragedy.'

He had, he said, visited England on many occasions before the war. He admired the English way of life, and his library contained the works of Oscar Wilde and a number of Shaw's plays. On one wall hung a large certificate recording his admission as a member of some institute or academy.

We were content to sit and listen to him; but in the end he apologized for keeping us up, and showed us to our beds. Stretched out in the voluptuous softness of a deep feather mattress, in the few seconds before I fell asleep I reflected on the contrast between that and our hard lying in the carbonari's hut the night before.

Next morning our host insisted on replacing some of our tattered clothing. From his own wardrobe he produced a jacket for me, some trousers for Toby, and for Michael a magnificent old coaching greatcoat complete with velvet collar and cuffs and beetle tails—a marvellous garment for the cold weather now upon us.

Such spontaneous generosity touched us deeply. Before we said goodbye, this excellent character walked with us for the best part of two hours to ensure that we took the quickest route through the mountains to our next destination.

6

After Firenzuola we entered the monastery zone, a stretch of the Apennines which approaches very close to the Adriatic coast, about twenty miles due west of

Ancona. Monasteries of various orders were dotted quite thickly about the countryside, and they were always good for a square meal and a warm, if hard, bed in a vacant cell.

Generally speaking, we were accepted with the utmost courtesy by the monks, although we did find that the degree of welcome varied considerably from order to order. The Benedictines were surprisingly grudging, but the Trappists, and in particular the order *Eremetici di Camaldolesi* could not have been kinder or more helpful.

All the monasteries seemed prosperous, with the monks living in the quiet calm of their retreat in startling contrast to the poverty of the surrounding peasantry. But we saw no sign that the peasants, happy in their squalor, were envious of them, and they undoubtedly did a great deal of good. We certainly found them most useful.

During this first week of October our number increased by one. At a farm that gave us accommodation for the night there was a brindled sheep-dog—a rarity in Italy and, I think, the first dog we had seen on our entire walk. He looked underfed and timid, but he had some nice points and appealing ways and, as Englishmen will, we made rather a fuss of the creature, feeding him with odd scraps as we ate our minestrone. That night he followed us into the barn and slept in the hay with us, and in spite of exhortations to 'go home' he was still with us next day after an hour's walking. He seemed quite determined to join us, and since there was nothing we could do about returning him, he was accepted as a fourth member of the party. He was probably given more to eat on that first day than he would normally have had in a month and a very happy dog he was. With an eye to the possibility of our luck with food running out, we gave him the rather grisly name of 'Spare Rations', or just 'Spare', a name to which he soon began to respond with eagerness.

Apart from our enjoyment of his company, we found 'Spare' a great asset when appealing for food or shelter. To the villagers, the advent of three English prisoners was unusual but not sensational; the addition of a dog was indeed something and proved the 'open sesame' to any house. 'Spare' marched with us like a veteran for over three weeks, but then he left us for a farmer's wife, who seduced him away with some delicacy we could not provide.

By 9 October we had passed through Tuscany and were in the province of Marche. The Apennines, as rugged and formidable as ever, still served as our main highway, and on a clear day we could probably have seen the sea as the east coast was only about twenty-five kilometres distance. But a perpetual drizzling rain reduced visibility to a few hundred yards and the grandeur of the scenery was hidden from us.

The country people were as helpful and generous as ever, but we were warned that the country ahead of us was sparsely populated and accommodation would become more difficult. We had been advised to make for the monastery on Monte Catria, a very high mountain with a huge cross on its summit; but as usual the Italian estimate of the time it would take us to reach it was wildly out, and it was not until late afternoon that we saw the cross ahead of us and started to climb towards it. The monastery lay somewhere on the other side of the mountain, and was still hours away. For the first time since leaving Mariano I had visions of us spending a night on the bare mountain! Darkness fell when we were still some distance from our destination, although we could see the huge outline of the cross against the night sky. Then, quite suddenly, the rain stopped, the clouds parted, and, as we stood on the summit beneath the enormous iron structure, a pale moon shone down over the countryside.

I shall remember vividly all my life that walk down into the shadowed valley. Behind us the cross stood silhouetted against the clouds scudding across the face of the moon, and we moved in a still silence broken only by the murmur of mountain streams. Gradually we became aware of organ music floating up from the depths below, and for some minutes we stood spellbound. I have never heard anything so beautiful; it is impossible to imagine a more perfect setting for those majestic chords. The music grew louder as we continued downwards, and presently we turned a corner and saw, less than two hundred feet below us, the lights of the monastery.

We were welcomed with grave dignity by a monk, who indicated that he was unable to converse with us, but in silence led us to a long sparsely-furnished room. There we were provided with wine and a very good meal. Afterwards Toby and I sat before a magnificent open fire while Mike was taken for an interview with the Father Superior. He told us later that a great part of their conversation was conducted in Latin. The old man had been most pleasant and had intimated that we might stay in the monastery for as long as we wished —until the Allies arrived, if necessary. Toby and I exclaimed in horror when Michael said,

'This place has much to recommend it. Some time spent in meditation in these surroundings would suit me admirably.'

'Don't be bloody silly! We might be stuck here for months.'

We argued about it far into the night, and at last persuaded Michael that the Allied armies, two hundred miles to the south, were still too far away for us to lie up and wait for them. He had a degree of self-discipline and patience which might have withstood months of inactivity and tension. Toby and I had not. In fact, I found our routine day's rest on Sundays more than I could bear, and by the end if it my irritability always taxed the patience of the other two. The contemplative life was definitely not for me.

Within the confines of the monastery was a small farm with outbuildings, and here a few laymen worked the land and tended the animals which belonged to the monks. We spent the Saturday and Sunday nights here, in the company of some very peculiar people. Five civilians, who had been released from an internment camp near Ancona, had sought refuge in the monastery immediately after the signing of the Armistice. Four of them had moved on shortly before our arrival, but the fifth was still firmly in residence. A large, friendly, motherly creature, she literally welcomed us with open arms; her lips parting in a wide grin, two rows of pearly white teeth gleaming against the pitch blackness of her face.

'My, but Ah sure am glad to see you all, boys. Come on in!'

Before we had recovered from our surprise, we found ourselves seated around a large wood fire in the kitchen and listening to a stream of conversation from our genial and voluble companion. Lena—I do not remember her other name—was embarrassingly proud of her status as a member of the British Empire. She had accompanied her husband, an Italian sailor, from the Gold Coast to Italy, but as soon as he set foot once more on Italian soil, he had disappeared and she never saw him again. Unable to produce proof of her marriage, she was on the point of being deported back whence she came, when war broke out, and poor Lena had spent the next three years interned as an enemy alien.

'Ah sure am looking fo'ward to the arrival of our troops. Boy, what a party Ah'm gonna have!'

Michael, Toby and I shared a large and rickety double bed, and, given the slightest encouragement, I reckon Lena would have been in there too. As it was, a bed companion in the shape of an Italian youth turned up, just as we were falling asleep. He had been sent by the monks, he said, and obviously imagined that this gave him licence to join us. We stared malevolently at him, and grudgingly made room at the foot of the bed. This turned out to be a mistake; I had his feet, which were none too clean, a few inches from my nose all night.

On Sunday it rained all day. Lena fussed around us, cooked an excellent meal, and mended our shirts and socks. She was a big-hearted soul and really seemed to enjoy doing it. During the afternoon we listened to an impromptu recital on the chapel organ, but although we were received with courtesy, we got the impression that our presence in the monastery itself wasn't welcome, and as soon as the concert was over we returned to the farm.

Monday morning came at last and we started our trek once more. Michael, I am sure, was as thankful as any of us to be on the road again, although it was probably the presence of the garrulous Lena, rather than the arguments of Toby and myself, that had convinced him that Catria was an unsuitable place for an extended stay.

Our original intention of keeping on walking until we met our own troops had not altered in the light of events. We had long since given up any hope that a spectacular Allied breakthrough was imminent; on the occasions when we found a house with a radio, the news was invariably depressing in the extreme. The whole advance had come to a halt, and the battle had deteriorated into a stalemate which would probably last the winter.

We discussed the possible alternative of turning towards the Adriatic coast and there, by theft or bribery, obtaining a boat and sailing south to a point beyond the Allied line; but the idea never really took root. The risks seemed disproportionate to the chances of success. We were secure in the mountains and saw no sense in sticking our necks out by moving down to the coast, straight across the German supply axis.

By the middle of October we were near Perugia, and had covered nearly two-thirds of the estimated distance we had to travel. We were all extremely fit still, and there seemed no reason why we couldn't cover the remaining two hundred miles without difficulty. But whereas our bodies were standing up well to the strain, our clothing was not. For some days now I had been walking without socks, having been forced to discard the tattered remnants clinging to my ankles. My boots still held out, but both Michael and Toby were having to pack the soles of theirs with newspaper and cardboard to stop the sharp stones cutting into their feet.

Food was still adequate, and shelter easy to find. The weather got no worse, and the country was, if anything, a little easier. But in spite of all this the adventure began to take on a different and less carefree aspect. Up to now, although a brush with the enemy was always a danger, our journey had been hard but not unpleasant apart from our meeting with the parachutist. The nearer we approached to our goal, the more the nervous tension rose. We were driven on with ever-increasing energy, burning up the land at a great pace, and feeling bitterly disappointed if each day's mileage did not exceed that of the previous day. As a result, our nerves gradually started to fray and outbursts of temper and obstinacy became increasingly common. We were inclined to be morose and annoyed with ourselves and each other.

In our journeyings so far we had met Italians in many walks of life—country folk, partisans, priests, monks and a poet, and they had all welcomed us with a spontaneous generosity which none of us will forget. But on 17 October, near the town of Norcia, we met with a very different reception. We carried out our routine reconnaissance to find a suitable place for the night, but instead of choosing a small farm, we settled on the largest and most imposing in the district. I can't really think why, unless it was that we were all heartily sick of the squalor of our usual quarters. The thought of another night '*nella fienile colle bestie*' suddenly became unendurable, and we were determined to sleep in comfort.

The place we chose, after a little searching, was a large, prosperous-looking villa, beautifully situated on the hillside; and we made for it quite openly, though with some trepidation. In the yard a bunch of farm workers were standing around a door at the rear of the house, apparently waiting for their wages. In the doorway itself stood a tall man with a shot-gun in his hand.

There was complete silence as we walked across the cobbles and we were aware of everyone's eyes upon us. The man with the gun looked less than welcoming, as we put our usual request. His reply matched his expression—a blunt refusal; but we were in no mood to retreat. We explained who we were and what we wanted. He showed no surprise.

'I am perfectly well aware who you are,' he said, 'and that is why you can't stay here.'

He continued to stand firmly in the doorway with the gun resting across his arm; while the farm workers gradually closed into a tight semi-circle round us. We looked straight at the padrone.

'Since you won't offer us any food,' I said, 'we're left with no alternative but to take it.' And with that we brushed past him and into the kitchen. Would he fire at our retreating backs, or not?

A few seconds later he followed us in. His mood had changed. He was obviously still anxious, but in a civil tone he offered us a meal, on condition that we left immediately after it.

'It is absolutely impossible for you to spend the night here,' he said.

We did not pursue the matter further but contented ourselves with a very welcome wash and brush up. The house seemed to contain a veritable army of servants, and Michael managed to grab one and ask her if it was on the phone. No, it wasn't, she said, and we breathed more easily for the knowledge. Our unwilling host, we felt, was quite capable of ringing up the nearest German post and handing us over. It was comforting to know that this possibility, at least, could be ruled out.

Now that we had time to look round, we saw that

the house was magnificent, and beautifully furnished and appointed. It looked as if the padrone was a man of means. Just before dinner we met his wife. She was smartly dressed, and she took in our dishevelled appearance with ill-concealed distaste; nevertheless, she spoke good English, and made conversation with us while we sipped cocktails and waited for her husband to arrive.

The situation had a certain bizarre irony, and beneath the perfect courtesy, the atmosphere was icy with suspicion. We had forced our company upon her; she didn't like us, and we didn't trust her an inch. In this mood, we were led to a long mahogany-panelled dining-room.

The meal, served by candlelight, was perfection. There were two unexpected touches, a bottle of Lea & Perrins Worcester Sauce among the other condiments, and a box of Player's cigarettes handed round with the coffee and cigars. Gradually we all relaxed and by the time we were on to our second cognac we were quite a cordial company. Our host and hostess listened with keen attention to the story of our adventures, their ungracious reception and our own boorish behaviour on arrival equally forgotten. It developed into a most enjoyable evening, and it was not very long before our host had said to us:

'You really must forgive my earlier attitude. I do apologize. But I should explain that I'm one of those Italians—rather rare I'm afraid nowadays—who were fervent supporters of Mussolini before he was deposed, and one doesn't change one's convictions overnight. In my view, Badoglio betrayed his country when he surrendered to the Allies and I detest him. I have no particular love for Germany; but, as I see it, Italy's greatest enemy in the future will be Communism, and, if the

Allies win, this country will have its bloodiest revolution in history. I'm certain of it—and that's why I hope for a German victory. So, you see, we're enemies. But for tonight let's forget that and observe a twenty-four-hour armistice. More cognac?'

He was, as we had guessed, a very wealthy man. A financier and industrialist, his main interests were in Trieste. He normally used the house we were in for about two months of the year; but after the Armistice he had moved south with his family to get away from possible trouble from Yugoslav partisans. His loathing of Communism was an obsession with him. But he was an honest man, he entertained us lavishly, and we accepted his word when he said that we need have no fear of being apprehended during the night.

However, we refused his offer of beds in the house, and slept in the barn. After he had gone, having stood by with a lantern while we settled down in the hay, we moved to another barn on the other side of the yard. Perhaps so much caution was unnecessary, but, as Michael said. 'You can never be too careful.'

We slept well and were undisturbed.

7

During those last two weeks of October the weather daily became worse. Autumn's high winds and driving rain gradually gave way to winter's leaden skies, night frosts and perpetual drizzle. Our clothing, which had been adequate while the sun shone, was no protection from the icy winds that blew with fury from the mountains. Shelter at night was imperative, if only to thaw ourselves out after the day's drenching in sleet and rain.

The prospect of months of such weather, stuck in some primitive mountain village, was really too much even for Michael, and we decided to abandon any idea of lying up just behind the Allied line, and attempt a direct crossing. I had one obsession, and that was to be home for Christmas; but we were all equally in a fever of impatience. Each day we drove ourselves to cover more ground; if we had been capable of it, I believe we would have gone at the double, so great was our longing to get the whole business over once and for all. The filthy food, the lice, and all the accompanying discomforts of our vagrant's life were beginning to depress me more than I was willing to admit, and my usual buoyant optimism suffered in consequence.

So far we had managed to get along without serious differences. Of course we argued; we'd have been a pretty dull lot if we hadn't; but we had always succeeded in settling major points of policy or direction amicably. This was partly due to the system, which we had instituted right at the start, by which one man was the leader for the day, and his decision was final. This worked admirably. It avoided interminable arguments each time the track forked, for example; and although the leader was not necessarily always right, there were no recriminations, and we contented ourselves with the thought that the alternative track, although probably easier and quicker, might well have led us into trouble.

But in those last weeks things became more difficult. The decisions of the leader of the day, instead of being accepted fatalistically, were constantly being challenged by the others; arguments followed and it gradually became clear that we should soon reach a parting of the ways in more senses than one.

I forget who was map-reading on 21 October, but we had reached a point on the mountain ridges north of the Gran Sasso of the Abruzzi and had to decide whether to take a track leading down the slopes on the eastern side, or another to the west. We stood and argued the point on the summit with the wind drowning our voices and the rain running down our backs. Michael and I agreed that the western track was the obvious route; Toby favoured the eastern route and nothing would make him change his mind. He was convinced that he was right and Michael and I were wrong; Michael and I were equally convinced that we were right. Neither side would budge.

'All right,' said Toby, 'you go your way and I'll go mine.' Without another word he turned and strode off down the mountainside.

'Don't be a fool, Toby,' we shouted. "come back!' But he gave no sign that he had even heard us.

'Stubborn bastard,' muttered Michael, as he and I took the other track.

A week or so later we had reached a point where the central mountain ridge started to break up. There were gaps in the continuity of the hog's back, stretches of flatter, easier country sometimes extending for ten miles or more. On this better going we pushed up our daily average to as much as thirty miles in a straight line; but the easier conditions brought compensating disadvantages.

To start with there was a lot more air activity; and I remember the thrill of seeing, for the first time for nearly a year, a squadron of Spitfires on patrol. Michael and I, up in the mountains, found ourselves looking almost vertically down on them as the sun glinted on their engine cowlings and they twisted and weaved above the valley road below us.

This brief sight of our own countrymen, so near and yet so far, was a great boost to our morale; it was the first sign that the end of our journey was approaching. From that day on we were often treated to the same spectacle. Of the Luftwaffe the only sign we saw was the odd single plane batting home at low level.

Enemy activity on the ground, however, was another matter. More and more of the villages we passed were occupied by the Germans; traffic on the roads, particularly at night, was considerable, and at the same time it became more hazardous for us to move in daylight. The wide valleys which we were now compelled to descend into and cross were dangerous areas which the Germans were preparing as part of their defensive line. According to local reports, they were rounding up every available male between the ages of twelve and seventy and forcing them to dig gun emplacements and weapon pits, not only on the lower slopes, but even quite high up in the mountains. This slave labour had spread an air of despondency and utter misery over the entire countryside. In the villages, women and children huddled together in groups, while the men had fled to the mountains to avoid being conscripted.

The desolation of such villages, seen in the dusk of a rain-sodden day, seemed to epitomise the futility of war and I felt terribly sorry for their inhabitants, caught up, willy-nilly, in its trammels. And their misfortunes added to our own. Food was desperately short; bread was non-existent; at best, our evening meal consisted of bean soup. It was only sheer nervous energy, an intense inner sense of purpose, that kept us going now. It was this that drove us on, cold, wet and famished as we were; we had reached the home straight and the bit was well and truly between our teeth.

We were now faced with the most momentous decision of our entire journey. We were only about forty miles from the battle-line and the question had to be faced: how and where should we attempt our crossing? To the east, the Canadians were advancing against stiff resistance along the coast road. To the west was the American sector; while the main bulk of Alexander's forces were deployed on the central front ranging roughly from Cassino through Avezzano and the Sangro river to Campobasso in the east. We reckoned our best chance lay in the mountainous central sector, rather than on either of the two low-lying flanks; and so we headed in a direct line towards Castel di Sangro, Opie and Campobasso. And all the time the battle-line was getting closer; we had no doubt of that when, from time to time, we picked up the low rumble of gunfire reverberating among the hills and borne to us on the wind. Our excitement grew each day, and the atmosphere became tenser than ever.

Then suddenly, there it was, at our feet. From the summit of a bald mountain that dominated the Sangro river we saw the flash of guns and the burst of shells. The valley opened out; to the south of it the mountain ridges rose again, silhouetted against the skyline; and these mountains were held by our own troops. It was an apocalyptic moment.

'With any luck,' Michael said, 'tomorrow should see us there.'

But were weren't there yet.

From our seat in the gods, we could see the problems set out before us too plainly: the German forward positions on the ridge, the flat valley which was an un-occupied no-man's-land; and between us and 'home' the river, and the road running alongside it. Somehow we had to get across them without being seen.

There was a village on the other side which we reckoned would probably be our last chance of getting any food. From then on the country was pretty well bound to be deserted except for the enemy.

On our way down to reconnoitre the road and river crossing, we saw an old man resting outside a small hut —a common enough sight during the last week or two. He looked like one of the itinerant shepherds who, normally much earlier in the autumn, drove their flocks down from the summer pastures in the mountains to warmer grazing plains below. These men were now left with the alternative of driving the sheep down until they reached the line, where they would be slaughtered by the Germans, or keeping them in the mountains until the snow came and killed them off anyway. It was a dismal enough set of choices, yet on the whole the shepherds preferred their flocks to die of exposure rather than provide mutton for German troops. So they had built stone shelters for them—and for themselves—and were prepared to stay beleaguered in the hills until the Allies arrived, or the winter ended.

This grizzled old chap looked typical of them; un-shaven, a high black felt hat on his head, and leaning on his crook, he watched us unmoved as we approached him. A younger man peered at us from the doorway of the hut. We hailed him in Italian.

'*Buon giorno, vecchio. Come va?*'

'*Va bene, grazie.*' It was the younger man who spoke. '*Da dove siete?*'

'*Siamo due ufficiali inglesi. Siamo scappati del campo de prigionieri e vogliamo ritornare alle truppe nostre.*'

Our Italian was getting pretty fluent by this time; but, as so often happens, the Englishman abroad, struggling with a foreign tongue, received his comeuppance.

'I must say this is a very pleasant meeting,' remarked the old man in the unmistakable accents of Camberley. 'I don't suppose you happen to have a map with you?'

Our astonishment must have shown in our faces, and he grinned at us.

'May I introduce myself—I'm Brigadier Valentine, late CRA of 7th Armoured Division, and this young man is my Italian guide. What are your names?'

Michael and I formally identified ourselves, and explained how we happened to be on that particular hillside at that particular moment. It seemed that we were all in the same boat. The Brigadier had broken out of the Senior Officers' Camp near Sulmona. He congratulated us on the distance we had covered and the good speed we had made. But the information he had to give us was hardly encouraging. Apparently there was a German tank laager just off the road, about half a mile down the track we were following. It was going to be difficult to slip through the lines unseen.

'But still,' he said, 'don't let me influence you. You appear to have done pretty well by yourselves up to now.' He had decided to stay put for a day or so and see how things progressed.

We felt that we should have a shot at this route all the same. If it proved too dangerous we could always retrace our steps.

'Goodbye, Sir, and the best of luck.'

'Goodbye. I hope we meet again under more pleasant circumstances.'

We left him leaning on his crook by the sheep-pen, every inch an Italian shepherd, every inch a British Brigadier.

We strode on down the steep track and soon came to the woods which bounded the road and river on either side, and in which, presumably, the Brigadier had seen the German tanks. We moved slowly and cautiously through the trees. We could hear an occasional vehicle as it sped down the road, but no sound of voices. The tank laager had gone, but not long before; bits of paper, empty cigarette packets and scraps of half-eaten food littered the ground alongside the road, and the track-marks were unmistakable. I picked up one of the discarded cartons. On it was printed '*Kamerad, kennst du Knackerbrot? Knackerbrot ist die Beste. Knackerbrot-Werke, Magdeburg.*' Apparently private enterprise still flourished in Nazi Germany.

We foraged around for as long as we dared, pocketing any edible scraps we could lay our hands on. I carried away a half loaf of black 'Berlin bread' and a small round Italian cheese, as hard as a cannonball and nearly as heavy. But I did not have them long. The river crossing was more difficult than we expected, for, after the heavy rains, the river was in half-flood. Wading across, with the water nearly to our waists, I lost my footing, and my precious cheese and bread went swirling down-stream. I was still struggling to rescue them when Michael started signalling frantically from the farther bank. I scrambled out of the river and had just gained the cover of the wood on the other side when a German convoy rumbled up the road not a hundred yards away.

I felt very sick about that cheese.

Progress was slow for the rest of the day. The weather, which had been crystal-clear in the early morning, deteriorated quickly and by midday it was raining incessantly. As we climbed higher, so the visibility became worse. At about four o'clock, cold, wet and hungry, we sat down in the shelter of a rock on the steep hillside and gazed longingly into a village spread below us. Smoke rose from the chimneys, and figures could be seen moving about. At least, it was not deserted, but whether the Boche were there we could not tell.

As we sat disconsolately pondering the situation we became aware of movement on the slope a hundred yards away to our right. We froze but it was only a girl of about fourteen, slowly driving her little flock of goats down to the village. We beckoned her over.

'*Sono Tedeschi quelli che passano?*'

She looked at us with wide, clear brown eyes.

'*Si, ci sono tanti Tedeschi qui*. But who are you?'

We told her.

'You must be very hungry,' she said, 'but you can't come down into the village. There are Germans in every house.'

She appeared to be deciding some problem, for she hesitated. Then she said:

'The best thing is for you to stay just here until after dark. Then I will come up and fetch you. You can stay the night in our house.' Perhaps she sensed our misgivings, for she added quickly, 'Don't worry, *Inglese*, I won't betray you.' With that she bade us '*Arrivederci*', rounded up her straying herd, and disappeared down the hillside.

We spent an anxious few hours by that rock, waiting for nightfall, and for the girl to return. It would be so easy for her to lead us straight into a trap. But she seemed a decent sort, and the prospect of warm food and shelter for the night kept us there in spite of everything.

8

For two hours we sat in the rain, and with every passing minute we grew colder and more miserable. Gun flashes lit up the night sky and the continuous sound of battle could be heard through the hissing downpour. So close were we to our destination that our fears of betrayal and recapture were multiplied; to fail now would be beyond bearing. What with the Germans so near, and the wet and the cold, and our suspicions of the girl, it was a trying wait.

Then, at seven o'clock, true to her word, the girl came back for us. She had crept out of her house under the very noses of the Germans, and in pitch darkness had climbed up the rocky mountainside and found us, without, apparently, the slightest difficulty. Calmly she proceeded to give us precise instructions as to what we were to do, and led us into the village.

German vehicles lined the main street, and from time to time when doors were opened we could see German soldiers inside the houses. Two of them passed us as we walked down the street, but they were too preoccupied with some discussion of their own to notice us in the darkness. Nevertheless my heart pounded and my mouth went dry, and the primitive instinct to turn and run had to be ruthlessly suppressed. It was partly the cool courage of our guide, who was, after all, little more than a child, that shamed us out of our panic and made us walk on without faltering.

We reached the house without further incident and were immediately installed in a room on the first floor. Here, sitting in darkness, we could keep an eye on the street outside. The girl, meanwhile, was cooking us a thick bean soup. The only other occupant of the house was her old grandmother, who could be heard weeping and complaining hysterically in the room below ours.

As we waited for the meal to arrive, fervently hoping that the old woman would not attract too much attention with her moans and cries, we saw two German troopers approach the house. There was a loud hammering at the door and a gruff command to open up. Immediately there was complete silence in the grandmother's room; then the sound of the girl's footsteps, and the front door creaking open.

Michael and I were ready to jump out of the window at the first sign that the house was being searched. But after a few moments we caught the old familiar word 'eggs'. We grinned sheepishly at each other—it was only a couple of Krauts on the forage. And not a successful one, either. After a long argument with the girl the Germans left, empty-handed, to try their luck elsewhere.

A few minutes later the girl appeared, quite unruffled, and set two plates of thick bean stew before us.

We fell on it like hungry animals. When we had downed it she pointed out the quickest way out of the village and into the shelter of the mountains, and then led us to a tiny outhouse filled with hay.

'You'll be quite safe here, but make sure you leave before it's light in the morning.'

It was sound advice; but when we woke the sun was already well up in the sky, and we spent an anxious ten minutes making our getaway from the village. Its culmination was a crouching scramble across a patch of open ground into the thick woods beyond, during which the seat of my trousers, worn threadbare by rough usage and the lash of the elements, received its *coup de grâce,* so that I reached the wood in the same state as the proverbial character who refused to lead trumps. In this draughty state I spent the next forty-eight hours.

We climbed for an hour to put ourselves out of danger, and then we met a party of three Italian youths who were also trying to cross the line to the Allies. The information they gave us was valuable, if discouraging. There wasn't a hope in the direction in which we were bound; there were Germans everywhere. The only chance was to go back and try farther east, the other side of Castel di Sangro.

Michael and I talked the matter over, and at last decided to take their advice and retrace our steps. It was a bitter decision, for a very few hours' walking would have taken us right into the firing line and we might well have spent the next night in the security of some Allied unit's mess. By turning back we should add at least two days to our journey: two more days of the rapidly deteriorating weather, two more days of dodging the ubiquitous Germans.

We skirted the village and re-crossed the river where

I had dropped my cheese the previous day. A long climb took us past the hut where we had seen the Brigadier, but whereas yesterday the sun had been shining, today it was cold, miserable and wet. Yesterday we had been chattering happily as we descended the hill; today we climbed it in grim silence. We were back-tracking, and it was deeply depressing.

We were still in this mood of frustration and annoyance when, clambering up the final slope of the mountain, we were confronted by an almost unbelievable sight. There, not fifty yards from us, and as delighted to see us as we were to see him, was Toby. It seemed incredible. Toby had walked off in a huff a hundred miles back, and here he was, as large as life, coming towards us as if we had parted at one end of Piccadilly and met again at the other.

He had a companion with him, a South African called Hal Becker, whom he had met the day after leaving us. He, too, had walked from Modena in the north, and at a most impressive pace considering he had a game leg, the result of a bullet wound in the knee collected outside Tobruk. He was slightly older than the rest of us and he had an air of determined toughness which made him a welcome new member.

Food was our worst worry. There were a fair number of small villages dotted up and down the valleys below us, but we didn't feel like risking a foray since the majority were sure to be occupied by the Boche. Our total stock of provisions was one very hard loaf of bread and a handful of walnuts, which was thin fare on which to tackle what was probably going to be the roughest forty-eight hours of the entire journey.

A couple of hours later, however, we were presented with what seemed manna from heaven, in the form of a flock of sheep conveniently penned within stone walls and watched over by a rather doleful and apathetic old shepherd.

'Help yourselves,' he told us, 'they'll all die of cold in a week or so anyway.'

We needed no second bidding. Within a few minutes a suitable animal had been lifted out and killed. The old man obligingly stripped, skinned and quartered the carcase for us. We cut half of it into smaller portions and boiled them in a large cauldron of dirty water in his stone shelter. When we left him an hour later we had a sizeable piece of boiled mutton slung about our persons.

The toughness of meat that has been killed one minute and boiled the next has to be experienced to be believed. Every mouthful we wrenched from the joint was a minor tug-o'-war. Also, freshly-killed meat unaccompanied by vegetables or bread or salt has a disastrous effect on the stomach. Within an hour I was doubled up with the most appalling indigestion, and would gladly have flung the rest of my share down the mountainside. However, I resisted the temptation, and throughout the afternoon the revolting and unwanted chunk of meat swung to and fro and struck me smartly in the small of the back at every step.

By four o'clock it was raining heavily again, and the temperature was dropping fast. The front, which had been moderately quiet all day, suddenly burst into life, and gunfire reverberated around the mountain tops like a distant thunderstorm.

We had reached a position on the ridge from which we could look down on to a five-mile stretch of the Sangro river. We could see Castel di Sangro, a fair-sized town, away to our right, and a road and railway that followed the river and led through half a dozen villages away to Rocavraso on the left. Each of these villages was packed with troops and transport, and, worse still, we could see through the gloom a whole army of men digging fortifications on the very slope we were standing on, not more than five hundred feet below us. We appeared to have landed plumb on the Germans' winter line, and a pretty formidable affair it seemed.

We stood there, a small, ragged and almost exhausted bunch of men, and surveyed the scene with sinking hearts.

It was at this point, if we had had more sense, that we should have called it a day, gone back ten miles or so, found somewhere to lie up for the winter and let the spring offensive roll over us. But in our tense and tired state this prudent alternative never occurred to us. Comfort, safety, food, everything we had been longing for, lay just across that gloomy valley and we were drawn to it by some force greater than ourselves.

'Well,' said Michael at last, 'that's it. We'll have a crack at it tomorrow. Now let's find some shelter for the night.'

Once again we were lucky. Way up in the mountains we found a tiny cottage, isolated and deserted, and after eating some more of our repulsive meat, we lay down huddled together in a corner. It was terribly cold; and for the first time on our journey I couldn't sleep. I lay there, staring into the darkness, praying that tomorrow would see a successful outcome to it all, and realizing just how tired, physically and mentally, I had suddenly become in the last twenty-four hours. I was still wide awake when the first glimmer of daylight showed through the open door.

We left the cottage early and made our way cautiously through the thick mist which enshrouded the whole landscape. The damp cold struck through what remained of our clothing and chilled us to the marrow. It was not a propitious start. We trekked slowly on, and after two or three hours came to the edge of a plateau. On the far side the slope dropped down through some woods to the river and a railway. We had to cross these; but somewhere between us and them were the German fortifications.

We had been moving to our left the whole morning in order to get as far away as possible from the main danger spot, Castel di Sangro, and the route had brought us to this large basin which we had not seen the previous night when we stood and surveyed the ground. The mist cleared, leaving a cold, sunny day and nothing could have looked more peaceful and harmless than the view ahead. The level plateau extended for about half a mile and beyond it a tree-clad slope fell away to the valley. It was uncannily silent and we could not detect the slightest sign of life or activity. All the same, it was potentially dangerous and we decided to attempt it in pairs, rather than run the risk of all four being caught in the open together.

As Michael and Toby set off, I shouted, 'Wait for us in the woods. We'll stay and see you over.'

Hal Becker and I sat and watched them; the two figures gradually grew smaller until, after about ten minutes, Toby disappeared into the shadow of the trees, followed a moment or so later by Michael.

Then Hal and I set out. At first all was quiet; but when we were about halfway across the open ground we heard the sharp crack of a gun-shot, followed almost immediately by two more. Instinctively we both started to run, and as we did so we saw a figure gesticulating to us and shouting. He held a rifle in his hand, and the green uniform he was wearing was undoubtedly German. He was standing at the edge of the wood about a hundred yards to our right.

It became a race for shelter. The German knelt down and took deliberate aim. As we reached the woods I heard two shots. One round went whining through the trees; the other hit Hal Becker and over my shoulder I saw him stumble and crash. I was running full tilt down a steep slope, and ahead of me, over the lip of a small crest, was what looked like some good dead ground. I hurtled downhill and leapt straight over it.

There was a sheer drop of ten feet; and at the bottom a German working party was digging a weapon pit. I landed literally in their laps. One of them raised a rifle and fired at point-blank range. I saw the movement and heard the shot, but felt nothing. Only when I tried to get up, I found my right foot would not respond. The Boche was still holding his rifle and shouting curses. I suppose he was as surprised and scared as I was. I lay and listened to his raving and gradually the sickening truth hit me hard between the ribs. After the months of trudging and hoping and the amazing freedom of our long trek through the heart of Italy, it was all over. I had failed at the very end, and was back exactly where I'd started—a prisoner of war.

EPILOGUE

Return to the Apennines

When I think back now, it seems to me that at that moment I grew up. I didn't know it at the time. At the time all I knew was an almost unendurable sense of disappointment, rage and frustration, an annihilating sense of failure. The desolation and misery were more profound than anything I had ever felt before, or, indeed, have ever felt since. They were heightened, I suppose, by pain and shock, for the German's bullet had broken my ankle.

During the following few weeks I was housed in a rudimentary prison hospital at Sulmona, where medical treatment was virtually non-existent. The wound went septic and I developed dysentery, so that I soon didn't care whether I lived or died. In the event I survived, and hobbling, thin and wretched, was shipped off in a cattle truck with hundreds of other POWs to Germany, to the vast camp at Moosburg which later became infamous for the 'great escape' and its brutal aftermath. From there I managed to make one more escape myself, but after a mere three days of freedom I was recaptured in Prague, and spent the rest of the war in the bag. But that is part of another story.

Michael and Toby were luckier than I. They succeeded in reaching and crossing the Allied line. Both survived the war, Michael to become a solicitor and a successful novelist and playwright, and Toby Professor of Military History in the University of Toronto. Hal Becker was killed in that fusillade of shots as he and I dived for the shelter of the wood. Of all the others who marched out of Campo P.G.49 that September afternoon which saw the beginning of our long march south, only a tenth, perhaps, succeeded in reaching the Allied lines or even remained free for very long. Most of the others were recaptured within days or hours, many of them without having moved from that initial laager in the dry stream bed. Quite a number were never heard of again. Some, no doubt, died of exposure or hunger in the mountains, while others were shot by German or Fascist patrols, and they have vanished without record from the history of the war, members of the company of forgotten casualties.

They, like the war itself, have already passed into legend, part of a world that seems almost as remote from ours as that of Lord Cardigan or the Duke of Wellington; why bother to try and recall from that remote era of one's youth such a modest and unheroic tale as this one? I first jotted it down soon after the war was over while I was studying for my finals in medicine, a page or two each night, almost as a form of relaxation. The events were still fresh in my mind, and I had the idea that it might be of interest if my children, like little Wilhelmine in Southey's poem, should ever say:

> 'Now tell us all about the war,
> And what they fought each other for.'

This was 'my' war, for what it was worth.

As I said earlier, I grew up during those moments when I fell headlong into that German weapon pit. I certainly wasn't grown up before, and, reading over what I wrote in 1947, I was sometimes tempted to soften the arrogance of youth and take the edge off the contempt I expressed so freely, especially in the early part, for the Italians. I don't find my attitude towards them particularly edifying, yet it seemed dishonest to pretend that I felt otherwise.

Like thousands of others, I was little more than a schoolboy when I went to war, and I am sure I shared most of the prejudices of schoolboys of that period, especially towards 'foreigners'. But those months of hard travelling, excitement and danger, with survival only made possible by the disinterested kindness of a great number of very poor people who had nothing to gain and a great deal to lose by sheltering and feeding us, knocked a lot of the certainties out of me. They gave me the rudiments of understanding and tolerance and a certain humility.

These things do not come all at once; but the sudden, total failure at the end of it all, when one was exhausted, physically and emotionally, did a lot to seal them into my mind, as if by shock treatment. It was largely as a consequence of those experiences that, after the war and repatriation, I decided to study medicine. I had never seen myself as a doctor before: afterwards, the choice was not difficult.

This makes it all sound dreadfully solemn and traumatic, and, taking the long view, I suppose that's what it was. In the short view, in terms of the experience as it happened to me at the time, it wasn't anything of the sort. It was, first of all, an adventure, a bit of a lark, and very much better than kicking one's

heels in a prison camp. Either way it was something I
wouldn't have missed for anything.

When I originally wrote it, it was the adventurous
aspect of it that was uppermost in my mind. I often
think how lucky we were—those who survived—the
young soldiers and sailors and airmen of that time.
Adventure and excitement were thrust upon us without
any bidding, and we were the richer for it. The young
today, sharing the same zest and curiosity, have to go
out and find these things for themselves; and I give
them all credit for their enterprise in doing so. It's so
much easier to stay at home, just as it was easier to sit
in prison camp than go through the effort and anxiety
to try and escape. But it was worth it.

Last year, for the first time since 1943, I returned
to the Apennines where so much of this story took
place, to stay with Eric Newby who had also been in
Campo P.G. 49, and who had later—as he has told the
story himself*—married his Wanda and settled in
Italy. The visit was not exclusively social; the
vendemmia, the grape harvest, was due to start in a
day or two, and any extra hand would be useful.

First, though, we spent a long day climbing one of
the peaks to the south of La Cisa. When we reached
it, we sat and munched our sandwiches with the great
sweep of mountains reaching round to Pietra Bismantova before us. I searched the superb panorama of
mountain and valley basking under the summer sun
for clues that might trigger off memories of that
journey of nearly thirty years before.

'That's Borgo Val de Taro down there', Eric said,
pointing to a barren little village clinging to the lower

* *In Love and War in the Apennines and Something Wholesale.*

slopes of Pietra Bismantova, 'and that's Prato beyond. You went through both of them. Do you remember them?'

Did I? I remembered the long blazing autumn days as we sweated through the foothills and up into the Apennines, and innumerable *paesetti*, some no more than tiny hamlets, in the smoky dusks as we came to the end of each long, footsore, dusty day and wondered each time what our welcome would be. But it was difficult to distinguish them, to attach to each some exact and certain memory. I said as much to Eric.

He murmured something, and then said: 'There's a woman from Borgo Val de Taro coming in to help tomorrow. She may refresh your memory.'

The vendemmia started early the next morning. There were about twenty of us altogether, two Englishmen and the rest *contadini*, peasants of both sexes and all ages. Working alongside each other, we began to strip the vines. It was hard, hot, exhausting work—at least, it soon exhausted me—and none of us had energy or breath for conversation. Steadily the bunches of ripe grapes collected in the baskets and were transferred into the waiting carts, and there was another empty basket waiting to be filled.

We worked without a break till nine o'clock and then stopped and moved into the shade for food and wine. After a few moments Eric brought over a tall, strong-featured woman and introduced her to me. She was in her mid-forties, dressed in black, with a headscarf and wooden sandals, the uniform of the Apennine *contadini*.

'This is the signora I mentioned yesterday,' Eric said. 'She moved here from Borgo Val de Taro.'

I asked her what had happened to make her leave,

and, hesitantly, she told me her story. One day in the autumn of 1943, when she was a girl of thirteen, three English prisoners, accompanied by a dog, had arrived at the village and asked for food and shelter. Her father and mother had made them welcome, and they had stayed for two days and then moved on. The next day a German patrol arrived. Someone had talked. They surrounded the village, but they went straight to the girl's house and shot her father and mother and her two brothers in front of her. She alone was spared.

'It was the Tedeschis' way of discouraging other people from helping escaped prisoners,' she said.

Three men, accompanied by a dog? I remembered 'Spare', the sheepdog, which had spent three weeks on the march with us—but there had been plenty of prisoners on the run at that time, and any three of them might have picked up a dog on their travels. I looked hard at the woman: what would she have looked like as a girl of thirteen? I remembered that other child who had helped us so fearlessly in the village swarming with Germans, but that had been much farther south and much later on. This one . . .? It was an oddly painful confrontation, as if, in not clearly and immediately recognizing her, one was somehow dishonouring her family who had been so brutally and callously murdered for helping us, or three other vagabonds like us. And yet, and yet . . .

I haven't changed much over the years, and I said to her:

'Do you remember me, signora?'

It was her turn to scrutinize me and see if she could match what she saw to the memory of those terrible days. At last she shook her head.

'No, signor, I don't remember you.'

She smiled a little sadly and said: 'I grew up hating the Tedeschi, but time softens all things. One must forget to live.'

She turned away then and in a few minutes we went back to the peaceful, arduous task of stripping the ripe grapes from the vines.